THE CONCEPT OF KARMA

Thinking about Life and Death

Ian Walker

Thomas & Mercer

Copyright © 2024 Ian Walker

All rights reserved

The right of Ian Walker to be identified as the Author of the Work has been asserted by him in accordance with the Copyright, Designs and Patents Act 1988.

The characters and events portrayed in this book are fictitious. Any similarity to real persons, living or dead, is coincidental and not intended by the author.

No part of this book may be reproduced, or stored in a retrieval system, or transmitted in any form or by any means, electronic, mechanical, photocopying, recording, or otherwise, without express written permission of the publisher.

Published by Thomas & Mercer, Seattle

Amazon, the Amazon logo, and Thomas & Mercer are trademarks of Amazon.com, Inc., or its affiliates.

ISBN-13: 9798321582572

Cover design by: Art Painter
Library of Congress Control Number: 2018675309
Printed in the United States of America

*To Noah
with love*

CONTENTS

Title Page
Copyright
Dedication
Abbreviations
Prologue
Chapter 1 — 2
Chapter 2 — 21
Chapter 3 — 31
Chapter 4 — 38
Chapter 5 — 46
Chapter 6 — 57
Chapter 7 — 70
Chapter 8 — 77
Chapter 9 — 89
Chapter 10 — 94
Afterword — 102
About The Author — 104
Books By This Author — 106

ABBREVIATIONS

A.U.   - Aitreya Upanishad
A.V.   - Artharva Veda
B.U.   - Brhadaranyaka Upanishad
C.U.   - Chandogya Upanishad
I.U.   - Isa Upanishad
K.U.   - Kansitaki Upanishad
Ka.U.   - Katha Upanishad
Ke.U.   - Kena Upanishad
K.V.U.   - Kathavatthu
M.U.   - Mundaka Upanishad
P.U.   - Paingala Upnishad
Ps.U.   - Prasna Upanishad
R.V.   - Rig Veda
S.U.   - Svetasvatara Upanishad
V.U.   - Vajrasucika Upanishad

PROLOGUE

I asked my brother, an eminent Australian cardiologist, what he thought of *karma*. He said: 'My karma's run over your dogma.' I asked my ten-year-old grandson what he knew of *karma*. He said: 'Isn't it where you get what's coming to you?'

There is doubtless truth in both responses.

In *The Concept of Karma*, I have tried to get behind common conceptions to the philosophical core of *karma*; notably, what to make of our own life and death. Or should that be: our own lives and deaths? As you will see in what follows, I argue that it is not the latter.

For the sake of simplicity I have not used diacritical signs in transliterated Sanskrit or Ancient Greek words.

Ian Walker
Oxon, 2024

The Concept of Karma

Ian Walker

Thinking about Life and Death

CHAPTER 1
Karma and History

'All extensive and enduring religions are coalitions of beliefs, practices and traditions. It may be desirable, for the sake of good order and statistics, to define the boundary of a religion as 'quod semper, quod ubique, quod ab omnibus creditum est' ('that which is always, that which is everywhere, that which is by all people believed'), but such a condition never has and never will exist' (*The Meanings of Death*, Bowker, 1991). In what follows, we shall see that Bowker is indisputably correct. Within different faiths, and even within the same faith, even the fact of diversity is itself differently interpreted. I hope that I manage to show something of that diversification, in regard to the doctrine of karma, in all its glory.

In Sanskrit, the language of the Hindu scriptures, *karman* (nominative: *karma*) means, simply, 'what is done', or 'deed', or 'act'.

Later, it came to mean 'the unseen potentials for future pain and pleasure which we accumulate as the result of good and bad action. Without exhausting these potentials there is no release from rebirth for the soul. Thus karma constitutes bondage in Jaina, Buddhist, and Vedic thought' (*The Oxford Companion to Philosophy*, 1991).

For those uninterested in the exegesis of Hindu and Buddhist scripture, the following part of this chapter may be overlooked.

The beginnings of *karma* can be traced back to the ritual sacrifice of the Vedic period (between c.1500 and 900 B.C.). There is not a little difference of opinion as regards the origin of the doctrine: 'Some have stated that it was borrowed by the Aryans from the primitive people of their new home, among whom a belief in the passing of the soul after death into trees, etc., was found' (*Outlines of Indian Philosophy*, Hiriyanna, 1932). The Aryans were invaders who came from the northwest to conquer India from the native (dark-skinned) Dravidians, or Dasyu, in about the middle of the second millennium B.C. The Aryans' religion and culture were related to that of the Greeks and Romans, and of ancient Iran.

The main components of Hindu scripture are the *Vedas* (the word itself means (sacred) knowledge), being sacrificial rituals administered by the Brahmin (priestly) class (the *Rig-Veda*, the *Sama-Veda*, the *Yajur-Veda*, and the *Atharva-Veda*) which are over 1,000 ancient chants, hymns and songs (dated anywhere between 1500 and 900 B.C.).

The *Brahmanas* are disputations on the nature of the sacrificial rituals belonging to the *Vedas*. It is difficult to overstate the importance of sacrifice which characterized the periods of the *Vedas* and, later, the *Upanishads*.

The *Aranyakas* and *Upanishads* record and express the search for knowledge and understanding of faith. The *Upanishads* enshrined metaphysical and religious doctrines that became the most important source of the theological thought of later Hinduism.

The *Bhagavadgita* (often simply called the *Gita*), the Song of the Lord, is, while separate, closest in concern and content to the *Upanishads*; it can be found in the epic the *Mahabharata* and may date to the second century B.C. (the other, great Hindu epic is the *Ramayana*).

The *Vedanta* – the end of the *Vedas* – is made up of commentary on the *Gita*, the *Upanishads*, and the *Vedanta Sutras of Badarayana*.

Of all these, the *Gita* is the central text. The *Mahabharata* tells the story of warring branches of the Kaurava family and in the *Gita* we find Arjuna, a younger brother, with a crisis of conscience: he cannot bring himself to kill his cousins. The *Gita* is the conversation between Arjuna and Krishna, who as Lord Vishnu's *avatar* (incarnation), debates with Arjuna the rights and wrongs, the duty (*dharma*), he has to fight. At first, Lord Krishna says, Arjuna is attaching a false importance to death because our embodied selves are eternal, they cannot die when the body dies:

'The Blessed Lord said: … Those who are truly wise do not mourn for the dead any more than they do for the living. Never was there a time when I did not exist – or you or these princes; nor will there be a time when any of us will cease to be hereafter. Just as the embodied selves pass through childhood, youth and old age in their bodies, so too there is a passing [at death] to another body' (ii.12).

Krishna then argues that, because of this, Arjuna should not hesitate to fight. He goes on to say: 'As a person throws away his clothes when they are worn out and puts on new ones, so does the embodied self cast off its old bodies and enter new ones.' According to the *Gita*, the way to overcome the accumulation of bad *karma* is not to withdraw from all life and action but to engage in appropriate action without attachment. Otherwise, the long continuation of rebirth (*samsara*) will continue and escape from this endless cycle (*moksha*) to *nirvana* will never be achieved.

Karma, then, is action with the implication of consequence: what we are is a consequence of what we have done (or failed to do) in the past; it is not a matter of rewards or punishment but the simple consequence of causation.

What we do now will create the circumstances that the soul (*jiva*) will inhabit at some point in the future. And this process is accumulative.

This 'simple' picture has generated an extraordinary amount of debate over the various questions it raises: in what form does the karmic causality of rebirths take place? Rebirth into a higher/

lower caste? Rebirth as a different animal? (For some this creates a hierarchy of animals). Is rebirth immediate upon death? Is there a gap? What determines such a gap? Does the *karma* of past lives accumulate in subsequent lives? Can the dying person influence the nature of his rebirth at his death? And so on.

Whole schools of Indian philosophy have grown up around these questions. I shall not, for the most part, pursue them in that they add not one whit to the basic questions that arise from the simple doctrine of *karma* that I have outlined.

The Vedas

To find the origins of *karma*, we need to look earlier, to the *Vedas*.

Others see *karma* as gradually evolved by the Indians themselves. It is first found distinctly mentioned in the *Upanishads* and, even among them, not all lay equal emphasis on it. All that can be said with certainty is that it had developed, and belief in it had spread widely, by the time of Gautama, the Buddha. Buddhism – and Jainism – took new shape outside the orthodox Aryan tradition. And while both emerged from a non-Aryan background, both were expressed through the medium of Aryan culture.

The karmic act is always first to be understood as the ritual act (see Van Buitenen, 'Dharma and Moksa', *Philosophy East and West*, Vol. 7).

In the *Rig-Veda* we find:

'7. Go forth, go forth upon those ancient pathways. By which our former fathers have departed. Thou shalt behold god Varuna and Yama. Both kings, in funeral offerings rejoicing.

8. Unite thou with the Fathers and with Yama, with *istapurta* in the highest heaven.'(*Funeral Hymn to Yama*, R.V. 1.10.14, see also A.V. 18.2.20; 11.1.36)

Here the departed are represented as united in paradise, not only with the Fathers and with Yama, but with the rays of the sun (R.V. 1.109.7), and with glorified bodies, while on earth.

'*Ista*', in classical Sanskrit, means 'charitable deeds' and denotes the gifts given to priests (*Religion and Philosophy of the Veda*, Keith, 2017). The point is that the merit resulting from these acts cannot strictly be termed ethical and that it was yet believed to precede the person to the other world, there to await his arrival, to secure bliss for him. A similar notion can be found in the *Artharva-Veda*:

'With my soul (*manasa*) I ascend to the great sacrifice as it goes dwelling in my austere fervour (*tapasa sayonih*)'.

Müller sees here a hint of the inner sacrifice which liberates the human being and enables him to rise beyond himself (*The Vedas*, 1956). This, however, seems akin to the idea that what we sacrifice here below we shall gain a hundredfold in heaven, thus removing the notion to that of the strictly ethical. But *istapurta* cannot be divorced from the original context of the sacrificial act. Atharvan, the sage, it is declared in the R.V. 'by sacrifices laid the paths' (1.83.5).

Istapurta has been described as the 'distant precursor' to *karma* (Keith, *op. cit.*). So, it is possible that we have here the germ of the later doctrine of *karma*, a word which in the R.V. means 'work' in general, or specifically 'sacrificial work'. Such works constitute the merit which wins bliss in heaven for the departed soul. It is necessary only to universalize the notion of work, making it apply to all deeds, and not just the sacrificial offerings, to get the fully-fledged doctrine of *karma*, as held in later times.

If the fruit of *istapurta* is reaped in heaven (R.V. 10.14.8), what of the fruit of other deeds? Those of extreme evil make the human being 'dig his own pit' (R.V. 11.29.6, 9.73.8-9, 7.104.3-17, 4.5.5). But what of those less significant transgressions to which we are prone?

All of us have neither just good nor just evil to our credit. It is certain that, according to the teachings of the *Vedas*, something happens to us after death. In one place we are told that the body goes 'somewhere' (A.V. 11.8.33); in another we are told that the 'soul' goes to the Fathers (A.V. 18.2.23); elsewhere the entity goes to the world of righteousness or paradise (A.V. 9.5.1-3, 12.13.17). But as to what happens wherever this 'person' goes is more doubtful. In this regard, we are told of the abandonment of disease and infirmities at the threshold of heaven (A.V. 6.120.1-3), and the making whole of the human being (R.V. 10.14.8). These might seem to suggest that all imperfections are abandoned at the threshold of heaven, but it does not entail their obliteration. There imperfections are discarded because it is only the 'whole' in body who reach heaven. This is probably only a figurative expression for those who are 'blind' – who have eyes but do not see – or those who are 'deaf' – to the call of the truth: 'The wicked travel not the pathway of law' (R.V. 9.73.6).

As to what happens to the wicked, we are not so sure. Some note the annihilation of the wicked at death, others see them as banished to a hell. The A.V. speaks of a home below the abode of the female goblins and sorceresses (*maraka loka*). A deep place is mentioned in the R.V. and is said to have been produced for those who are evil, false and untrue. References to this type of 'end' could be multiplied and could be variously exegeted: the 'pit' (cf. *sheol* in the Hebrew Old Testament) or the 'home below' may be a kind of hell; it may be a place of annihilation, or it may be figurative about immediate consequences of evil, although the latter is unlikely.

Heaven or hell (or the pit, abyss or annihilation) are in themselves ideas of reward and punishment although originally they may not have been considered in that light. Heaven is the world of what has been well accomplished (*sukritasya lokani*) (A.V. 6.120.1). It is regarded as the reward of those who practise rigorous penance (*tapas*), of heroes who risk their lives in battle (R.V. 10.154.2-9), but above all of those who bestow liberal sacrificial gifts (R.V. 1.125.5; 10.107.2).

The A.V. is full of references of blessings accruing to the latter (so MacDonnell, *Vedic Mythology*, 1897). These, as noted in regard to the cremation right, Agni takes to the other world, of the Fathers, and of the Gods (A.V. 10.16.1-4). He places the mortal in highest immortality. Whether the dead go to the world of the Fathers, or that of the Gods, is not at issue here. But these two may be regarded variously as separate, or different, or the same place (A.V. 1.31.7).

Of all its appearances in the *Vedas, karma* never appears in the sense of fruit of work (*phala*). The development of work to include fruit of work was not very difficult, but took place at a later date. (An important point to note here, especially in connection with later developments, is that *punerjanman* (transmigration) does not occur in the *Vedas*. But the participles *punah punarjayamana* 'being born again, again' does; and *navonavo jayamanah* 'being born anew, a new' is applied to the moon (R.V. 10.85.19) and these point in the direction of the later uses as technical terms. Otherwise, it is only applied to recurring phenomena of nature anthropomorphically described (R.V. 10.16.3; 10.58.7). The *Upanishads* ascribe to the R.V. the artificial manner in which this is done; this favours the view that here we have to do with a doctrine of recent origin for which a confirmation was sought in the ancient sacred texts (see for example, B.U. 1.4.10; A.U. 5.2.4).

This brief survey is sufficient to enable us to construct an example and model of a possible life/death of an Indian of the Vedic period. The following points need be noted in this model:

1) There is a causal relation such that action A, being *istapurta*, will be followed by effect B, the accrual of these gifts in heaven.
2) From the above it follows that there is an afterlife which may be enjoyed.
3) The nature of this afterlife is unclear: it may be with the Fathers, with the Gods, with Yama, with the sorceresses and female goblins of the home below; it may be in the pit or abyss, or, as Roth argues, it may be of sufficient duration only to enable the annihilation of the person in the abyss to take place.
4) The causal effect of the accrued blessings of the *istapurta*

should always be understood as issuing from the sacrificial context; this cannot be extended to cover all action.
5) To determine whether there is a hell and whether or not those who are sent there (and who sends them) are so sent because of actions divorced from the purely sacrificial context and of a more general and ethical nature, is hard to determine.
6) From the above it can be seen that the *Vedas* know nothing of the idea of transmigration; and the idea of recompense for action in the present is not to be found in the *Vedas*.

Let us now assume there existed, in the Vedic period, two people named Brown and Smith. Every day, Brown had participated in the *istapurta* and was liberal in his gifts of sacrifice. Upon his death, he was rewarded with life in the land of the Fathers and Gods and there joined his *istapurta*, which secured his bliss. On the other hand, Smith had never built up *tapas*, never offered sacrifice, never fought in battle, and on top of that had killed his aunt Fanny because he disliked her cooking. Upon his death, Smith was sent to the world below and suffered at the tortuous hands of the female goblins (or alternatively was annihilated in the abyss).

There is little (given the assumption that *istapurta* is causally efficacious and that there is a life after death) that seems to present immediate problems. It appears at first as though we have here a simple causal relation, effective in the afterlife. Something of a problem presents itself though when an additional factor is added, i.e., Brown's knowledge that he will in (say) 20 years' time (let us say he is now 60 and will certainly be dead by then) be enjoying the bliss provided by his *istapurta*. Or, conversely, that Smith knows he will be punished for his evil life and disregard of the sacrifice. So, at T^1 Brown knows that at T^2 (20 years later, or x years later: '20' may be regarded as a variable) he will be doing action B (enjoying his secured bliss). This entails a certain kind of foreknowledge. Some would say that Brown doesn't really *know*, he merely *believes*. Yet in this model we are assuming that Brown is correct, and that, because *istapurta* is causally efficacious, and can be known, then he will at T^2 be enjoying its fruits.

A good many contemporary philosophers have held that a proper application of the verb 'to know' requires not only that the knower holds a true belief, but also that he has evidence or grounds for his belief. Consider the fortune-teller who 'sees' future events in her crystal ball. She gets it right every time; she makes no mistakes in 10,000 tries. Assume also that the crystal ball-gazer is not permitted to know her record. In this situation, there is nothing that could be counted as grounds or evidence for her beliefs about the future. Still, if she got it right every time, we would have to admit that she *knows* what is going to happen in the future; though we might also have to admit that we do not understand how this knowing device works. This could provide something of a *prima facie* logical incompatibility. For if Brown knew yesterday (T^1) that he will perform a particular action at some time in the future (T^2), then Brown's knowledge is past and being past it is unchangeable and so necessary. If Brown knew at T^1 what will happen then it cannot now be the case, or at any time in the future be the case, that he did that not know at T^1 what will happen. Nothing can happen to make him not know. But if a proposition p is necessary, and p entails q, then q is necessary. The action in question, being foreknown by Brown, is necessary and so not free.

Another problem associated with such 'knowledge', some would argue (see e.g. A.N. Prior, 'The Formalities of Omniscience', *Philosophy*, 1962), is that if Brown exists that T^1 he can only know what is true at T^1. So that with respect to an action occurring in the future relative to T^1 (i.e. T^2) the claim that the action will be performed at T^2 is not true at T^1; this is so because the claim that the action performed the T^2 is neither true nor false at T^1. As the doctrine of *karma* is developed, these problems become more acute and present a real difficulty as regards freedom/determinism in the Indian doctrine. I will consider this later.

The Upanishads

As noted earlier, the *Upanishads* present a more developed understanding of *karma* but are nonetheless difficult to interpret. I will not argue about the nature of the *Upanishads* as a corporate body of literature with a thoroughly synthesized teaching (which I do not believe to be the case) but will examine those passages from some of the so-called 'Principal *Upanishads*' which I consider most obviously deal with *karma*. Dating the *Upanishads* is an extremely difficult task for it is likely that all have undergone a long work of redaction and rearrangement. Of the *Upanishads* to be dealt with here, there are only two which seem definitely to be pre-Buddhistic viz., the *Brhadaranyaka* and the *Chandogya*. It will not be claimed or assumed that the other *Upanishads* are post-Buddha documents, but they do at least seem to be later.

Brhadaranyaka Upanishad

Early in this work (B.U. 1.5.15) we find mention of three worlds: of men, of the Fathers, and of the Devas. The former is gained by progenitation, the latter two by sacrifice. Little difference can be seen between this idea and that of the *Vedas*. So-called rebirth texts do not appear in the B.U. until we come to the '*Yagnavalkya*' sections (B.U. 3-4). Here, already, familiar ideas are found which give expression to the thought of the soul's transmigration, and transfer retribution from the future world (as found in the *Vedas*) to the present:

'Yagnavalkya said: "Take my hand, friend. We two alone shall know of this. Let this question of ours not be discussed in public." Then these two went out and argued, and what they said was *karman*, what they praised was *karman* viz. that a man becomes good by good work, and bad by bad work...' (B.U. 3.2.13).

Here, some believe, that what is intended is that *samsara* continues by means of *karma* and man's inborn character is the fruit of his previous existence. This interpretation assumes *samsaric* existence but it is difficult to see that the passage will really allow this. That after a person's dissipation a man becomes good by good work etc., does not entail that he is reborn. However, that *karma* is now understood as a causal relation where by good work (the effects of a 'good man's' results), a man becomes good, *is* entailed.

Yagnavalkya expresses himself more clearly in another well-known passage:

'3. As a caterpillar, drawing near to the tip of the blade of grass prepares its next step and draws itself up towards it, so does this self, striking the body aside and dispelling ignorance (*avidya*), prepare its next step and draw itself up (for its plunge into the Brahman world) ... In proportion as a man acts (*karma*), as he behaves, so does he become. Whoso does good, becomes good; whoso does evil, becomes evil. By good works (*punya karma*) a man becomes holy (*punya*), by evil (works) he becomes evil.

'But some have said: "This person consists of desire alone. As is his desire, so will his will (*kratu*) be; as is his will, so will he act (*karma*); as he acts, so will he attain.

'6. On this there is this verse:

To what his mind (and) character (*linga*) are attached,

To that attached a man goes forth with his works (*karma*).

Whatever deeds he does on earth,

Their rewards he reaps.

From the other world he comes back here,

To the world of deed and work (*karma*)' (B.U. 4.4.3f).

Verses 3f could quite possibly be understood as containing no reference to transmigration but be simply about the entrance from an earthly to a heavenly or hellish life. However, it is difficult to make sense of verse six ('from the other world he comes back here...') outside the context of transmigration within the realm of *samsara*. This understanding also gives sense to the caterpillar image in verse three. The verse is almost certainly a later addition (so Deussen, *Philosophy of the Upanishads*, 2020). The passage does not recognize a twofold retribution within its karmic structure, in a future world and again upon earth, but only one (as verse six probably indicates) by transmigration. Immediately after death, the soul enters a new body, in accordance with its good or evil deeds. It seems then, that for *Yagnavalkhya*, retribution is seen in the form of one rebirth in the sphere of empirical reality. In place of the ancient Vedic recompense in the other world, there is recompense in transmigration. This view seems to me to make best sense of the passage which, I think, becomes extremely difficult if seen, as Vedic passages are, to be about recompense in a fixed, future world only.

A further text of great importance is B.U. 6.2 (cf. also C.U. 5.3.10) which is most difficult to understand as anything other than in a setting of transmigration and *samsara*. This text teaches a double retribution: once by reward and punishment in the other world, and again by rebirth upon earth. This feature appears to be primitive and represents the combination of the future recompense found in the *Vedas*, with the recompense of the transmigration doctrine. This text is found only in an appendix (*khilakandam*) and not in the two chief divisions of the *Upanishad*: the *Madhukaandam* (B.U. 1-2) and the *Yagnavalkhyakaandam* (B.U. 3-4). The similarities with C.U. 5.3-10 show borrowing or an earlier source from which both materials were drawn. When these two were collected, and later combined, it was likely that the appendix was still unknown, otherwise its original omission (when later it gained the admission which its importance demanded) is inexplicable. The text is therefore of late origin and a secondary product, which is further borne out by its contents.

A further text which complicates the hitherto simple causal efficacy of *karma* is B.U. 6.4.12 where in the procreation ceremonies concerning a curse on a man's wife's lover, the celebrant (the husband) is able, by means of the sacrifice, to nullify the pleasant karmic rewards due to the lover because of his (the lover's) sacrifices and good deeds which have accrued to him.

This line of thought is representative of the B.U. 4.4.3d where: 'Whatever deeds he does on earth, their rewards he reaps' (on earth), as the next line of the verse shows. Here the retribution is seen as the subsequent life that transmigration effects. Here one's life's fate is the consequence of one's prior *karma*.

Other Upanishads

I.U. 2-3 provides a more difficult interpretation than do the previous examples, but seems to indicate, in the ritual context, that there operates a karmic causality which determined some form of retribution. The following *Upanishads* can all be seen, on immediate perusal, to fit the models hitherto described: K.U. 1.1.6; 1.2.18; 1.3.7; 1.3.9; 11.2.7; M.U. 1.2.10; P.U. 1.9; 2.11; 3.2; 4.4; S.U. 5.7; 5.11-12.

Many *Upanishads* show a development whereby the karmic causality proves a burden and the reader is encouraged to escape the samsaric cycle. Others show a further development whereby the accumulated merit is seen as itself causally operative and this in turn produces further effects.

So, in the *Upanishads* we find various models of *karma* at work, all developing from the normative conception of *karma's* function as a basis where *karma* is to merit as cause is to effect. This notion is extended to the idea where in the V.U. 7: 'Good men perform works impelled by their past *karma*'. Here one's life's fate is the consequence of *karma* produced by all one's past actions. Here *karma* represents a type of metaphysical force, itself causally efficacious.

According to all these various models, every volitional act may produce a separate retribution (so *Buddhism and Society*, M. Spiro, 1970). The accumulation of these acts may bring about a retribution (say, in the form of a lower birth) or the accumulation of these acts may itself form a causally effective force which in turn brings about retribution (which may, of course, entail an infinite regress).

The Kathavatthu Debates of the Pali Canon

The Kathavatthu alone of the works of the Pali Canon is directly concerned with conflicting views within the Buddhist community. The Pali Canon is the collection of scriptures in the *Theravadin* Buddhist tradition, as preserved in the Pali language; it is the most complete extant early Buddhist canon and derives mainly from the *Tamrashatiya* school. It represents, perhaps, the apotheosis of philosophical reflection on *karma* in classical times. A number of these views revolve around the issue of *kamma* (*karma*). The general school in which the debate takes place is the *Theravada*, and that was made up in turn with groups of different philosophical persuasion. One such group was the *Puggalavadins*, or 'personalists' who, contrary to the main school of thought (the general canonical view is expressed in *Sutta Pitaka* that there is no permanent soul which is reborn), believed that a personal entity or 'soul' (*puggala*-person) exists. This *puggala* was not the same as the 'five aggregates' (see *The Kathavatthu*, S. Aung and C.A.F. Rhys Davids, 1915), which were previously seen as ever-changing and thereby allowing for rebirth, but it no doubt was similar. Without the existence of the *puggala*, *kamma*, the *Puggalavadins* argued, could not operate. Otherwise, the identifying of the same person from one life to the next would be impossible (K.V.U. 1.1.158ff). The protagonist and the antagonist then argue that ethically good and bad deeds exist (K.V.U. 1.1.160). The argument then returns to the nature of the 'person' and whether or not the *Puggalavadins*' interpretation allows empirically for such phenomena as death and the destruction of life. At issue here is not the metaphysical question regarding the existence of the soul; that is taken for granted. The conclusion drawn by the *Puggalavadins* in answer to the question is that phenomenology is extremely limited here because the soul is ineffable (K.V.U. 1.1.198). As the issue deepens, the *Theravadin* notes the fact that there is action (*kamma*) which produces an effect in a future state but that this does not entail that *the very same person* transmigrates from one existence to the next.

Another group are the *Andhakas* who debate with the *Theravadins* about the results (*vipaka*) or, as they have been called to date, the effects, of *kamma* (K.V.U. 7.8.1f). The issue in this section concerns the controverted point that old age and death are the result of action (*kamma*). This introduces then the problem as to which actions rate as karmic and which do not. *The Kathavatthu Kamma Debates*, J.P. Mc Dermott, 1975, quotes the commentary: 'The commentary clarifies this point, noting that *kamma* exists as a causal relation (*paccaya*) between (*akusala*) action and physical decay, but that the term "*vipaka*" refers only to mental results.'

The *Theravadin* states that there is a distinction between the physical and the subjective, only the latter being considered *vipaka* of *kamma*, while the *Andhaka* seems to maintain the categories as separate (K.V.U. 7.7). In this section about Earth and *kamma*, it is noted that inasmuch as there is human action directed to gain dominion and sovereignty over the soil, the earth itself is a result (*vipaka*) of such *kamma* (so the *Andhaka*). The *Theravadin*, however, attempts to show that land has nothing in common with the sentient results which are caused by *kamma*; that such results are a matter of subjective individual experience.

The debate over what *kamma* is, and what it is not, is extensive. As already noted, the *Theravadins* spoke of subjective experience only as appropriate *vipaka*. Others spoke of land, sound, sense organs etc. Probably the most representative view of the K.V.U. is the classification of *kamma* as found in the *Abhidhamma* where *kamma* refers to volitional action, of which there are three kinds: good (*kusala*), bad (*akusala*), and indeterminate or neutral (*aryakata*). Good *kamma* produces merit (*punna*) for which there is favourable or pleasurable retribution (*vipaka*), while bad *kamma* produces demerit (*apunna*) for which there is unfavourable or unpleasant retribution (*vipaka*). A rule of thumb would be then that all actions are karmic except those which may be considered ethically neutral, hence without effect (*vipaka*). That this is a rather loose rule is not hard to see and that debate would arise regarding what is or is not ethically neutral gives much of the K.V.U. its *raison d'être*.

Then there is the problem, which I mentioned earlier, of the infinite regress entailed by some views of *kamma* into which the *Andhakas* slipped (K.V.U. 7.10). They maintained that the result (*vipaka*) of past *kamma* are themselves the cause of further resultant states. In this regard, McDermott notes: 'Although they (the Andhakas) deny that their position implies an infinite regress of result entailing result entailing result, and so forth, the fear that such an implication is latent in their view is a prime reason for the Kathavatthu's rejection of the Andhaka interpretation of reciprocity as this relationship applies to results. If results perforce entail further results, an endless chain of cause and effect is created which precludes the possibility of escape from the samsaric round of existence. This, of course, would run counter to the entire thrust of Buddhism. Moreover, such a view comes dangerously close to the opinion that the present is merely a series of effects without personal initiative. To accept such a view is to negate the validity of any notion of free will and individual moral responsibility, such as is insisted on in the suttas' (*op. cit.*).

The *Andhakas* refuted such criticism by arguing that *kamma* operates only on a spiritual level. The counter to this argument would be to note that the cause/effect sequence is not result entailing result, but action entailing retribution. That Jones was killed by x is not itself something causally detrimental to his future rebirths. His was not good or bad action. This was ethically neutral (*aryakata*) action in which he was being acted upon, receiving retribution. Likewise, it might be argued, that if retribution had (for Jones) taken the form of a lower rebirth to, say, a very low caste, that *in itself* is not detrimental to his future rebirths: he has the same opportunities in his 'new state' of effecting only good deeds and thus improving his karmic status (it is difficult indeed to see how, if the rebirth is in the form of, say, a worm in the belly of a dog, that the worm might be able to act in such a way as to improve its karmic status! Presumably, being 'worm-like' is not particularly worthy of *kusala karma*).

This question was but one aspect of a broader controversy as to whether or not *kamma* was necessary. In the face of the normative theory which insists that the karmic consequences of merit can attach only to the actor himself, Buddhism has long sanctioned two practices which significantly qualify this theory: these are merit-sharing and merit-transfer. Here, put simply, one person can enhance the *kamma* of another. This can be done in many ways, some of which are viewed mechanistically, some (by the more sophisticated), are demythologised.

To return to our case history: Smith kills aunt Fanny. Because of this terrible deed his family offer oblation, and build pagodas, and help the poor etc., the sum total of which built up sufficient good *kamma* to outweigh his bad. But how can this karmic build-up be transferred (cf. B.U. 6.4.12)? I can see no way that the causal mechanism can be shifted from his relations to Smith that will not entail thoroughgoing cosmic determinism (where the karmic causes of one person affect others) than: at the sacrifice, etc., Smith (in spirit form of course) is in some way present and can participate in the offering, thus building up his own karmic supply of good and neutralizing his bad deeds. But these ideas seem to be the result of a psychological press.

Following Weber, it would be fair to say that many, if not most, sociologists of religion have seen the primary function of the belief in *karma* as providing a solution to the problem of theodicy. Weber notes, 'Karma doctrine transformed the world into a strictly rational ethically determined cosmos; it represents the most consistent theodicy ever produced by history' (*The Religion of India*, 1958), and again, 'The combination of cast legitimacy with karma doctrine, thus with the specific Brahmanical theodicy – in its own way a stroke of genius – plainly is the construction of rational ethical thought and not the product of any economic conditions. Only the wedding of this thought product with the empirical social order through the promise of rebirth gave this order the irresistible power over thought and hope of members and furnished the fixed scheme for the religious and social integration of the various professional groups and pariah tribes'.

To be sure, this has become one of its functions. But whether it was that which prompted such 'rational' considerations, or is its primary function, is another question. In a nutshell, the point is this: by separating the notion of *karma* from that of merit and by ignoring the motivations of the religious actors themselves, one might well arrive at the conclusion that the primary function of *karma* is to produce a solution for the problem of theodicy. I shall consider the question of theodicy below. Isolated from the idea of merit, the *karma* doctrine seems to be estranged from the future (which was the original motivation in *istapurta*) and isolated to the past and the present; that is, it serves to explain the present by means of the past and since one of the characteristics of the present is the differential and inequitable distribution of status and privilege, it provides a compelling solution to the theodicy problem. However, the doctrine of *karma* is inextricably related to the idea of merit, and is important precisely because of its lawful and predictable relationship to merit.

When the doctrine of *karma* is studied as a belief of religious people, rather than as a doctrine of religious treatise, it becomes evident that this doctrine was 'cathected', not because it explains the present only (i.e. suffering, evil, inequality) by reference to a past, but because it offers promise of affecting future rebirths by present action. The dominant motive (or psychological press) is not to discover the 'meaning of theodicy', but to do something about one's own suffering/predicament. Moreover, it is because the doctrine of *karma* precludes the possibility of alleviating *present* suffering – not because it is defective in explaining it – that there has developed an ideology which subverts the *karma* explanation for suffering, not better to explain it, that this doctrine has been reformulated in some circles to permit the neutralization of demerit and provide the sharing and transfer of merit. It should be better seen then, that *karma* is fundamentally soteriologically motivated, than as providing a solution to theodicy. So, to believe in merit, *karma* and rebirth, is to believe that, regardless of its magnitude, one can overcome present suffering and achieve salvation in the future. It can readily be seen that this whole idea of *karma* is ethical and on the assumption that the world is ethically meaningful, the seemingly inequitable distribution of good and bad fortune is in itself for many who hold a belief in *karma,* a convincing argument for the doctrine's truth.

There is ongoing debate about whether karma is a theory, a model, a paradigm, a metaphor, or metaphysical. Indeed, it is all these things depending on who you talk to!

Like all religious doctrine, *karma* is subject to not a little debate and disputation, inevitably entailing equivocation and, at times, mystification.

CHAPTER 2

Karma and the Person

We have seen how the *Kathavatthu* debates the question of whether there is such a thing as a soul. I shall look at the problems associated with this question below. But before we ask about 'souls', we should examine more pressing questions, such as: How do we identify a material object as a person? How do we individuate one person from among many? How do we identify the man from the boy? How do we identify a post-mortem person with the pre-mortem individual he is supposed to be?

Even though not one cell in my body was present when I was a child, I am still *the same* man who was that child. And it is bodily continuity that must be the main candidate making that identification possible. Indeed, some would say it is the *only* candidate.

There have been two main competing contenders for determining personal identity: one, the bodily criterion and, secondly, that the set of memories he has is necessary for bodily identity through time. John Locke (*Essay on Human Understanding*, Book II, Chapter 27, Section 15) is a famous protagonist of the second view.

The idea of a disembodied post-mortem survival logically depends on the view that the bodily criterion is not essential. As Penelhem says: 'If the identity of a person is necessarily connected with the persistence of his body through time, then it is logically impossible for a person to survive the death of his body' (*Survival and Disembodied Existence*, 1970).

If, on the other hand, personal identity is dependent on memory, and not bodily continuity, then a post-mortem person might be said to be identical with a pre-mortem person because of the memories he has. But here a lot of unpacking needs to be done: can I have memories without also having a body? How could such disembodied memories be identified?

In order to further his case for memory-identity, Locke offers two examples of 'puzzle cases':

'i) Should the soul of a prince, carrying with it the consciousness of the prince's past life, enter and inform the body of a cobbler, as soon as deserted by his own soul, everyone sees he would be the same *person* with the prince, accountable only for the prince's actions' (Section 15).

'ii) Had I the same consciousness that I saw the Ark and Noah's flood, as that I saw an overflowing of the Thames last winter, I could no more doubt that I who write this now, that saw the Thames overflowed last winter, and that viewed the flood at the general deluge, was the same *self*... than that I who write this am the same *myself* now whilst I write... that I was yesterday' (Section 16).

The first case involves that of a person who has 'acquired' the body of a contemporary. The second, someone 'sees' events that took place many years before his birth. The first represents personality transfer, the second apparent reincarnation. I shall not investigate other, apparently related, phenomena: mediums, ghosts, etc. Having said that, I believe that what can be said about disembodied persons can equally be said, *mutatis mutandis*, about ghosts, etc.

Here we are saying that disembodied existence is possible; that personal identity might continue without a body. It is only if the concept of survival is coherent that any sense can be attached to these, and other such, phenomena. In other words, I believe that this is primarily an epistemological issue.

What predicates can apply to being a person and can these predicates be applied to being a post-mortem person? In understanding the question of *sense* in this respect, one is speaking of the *attenuation* of predication. If 'has a body' is a predicate essential to being a person then no disembodied being can be a person, let alone one identified with a pre-mortem being.

Persons can move, interact, talk, snooze, scratch their noses; disembodied 'persons' is cannot.

Some might wish to ascribe to him (the disembodied person) perception, volition or even agency. But all of these will have to be greatly modified in the absence of the body: thinking, without a brain, for example, will need to be expressed differently. One way of doing this might be to say that predicates can be applied to Jones^b – the disembodied, post-mortem state – because he inherits from Jones^a – the embodied, pre-mortem state – some understanding of what these predicates mean.

What might our principal candidates for these predicates be? The prime contenders for such predicates seem to be those of perception (the disembodied person is believed to perceive what is going on) and agency (the disembodied person is believed to continue to have experiences). These are the principal predicates that seem to preoccupy those who wish to speak of disembodied persons.

In the case of embodiment, perception consists largely through the operation of the senses.

Let us take *sight* as our paradigm sense. I shall not consider all the sense organs here. What can be said of sight applies, *mutatis mutandis*, to all the others. Can a disembodied person reasonably be said to see? He doesn't have eyes. What sense of seeing within the visual field can be made of the verb 'to see' without the existence, let alone the operation, of the visual organs? Here the obligation falls on the proponent of the disembodied person hypothesis to give some meaning or context to the talk of seeing what one cannot look at.

Post-Cartesian epistemology may offer a way out in speaking instead of having certain visual experiences. This might be fleshed out by, say, suggesting that a disembodied person 'sees' in much the same way as a normal observer from a particular spatio-temporal spot, or realm. No sense applies to the notion of seeing from no point of view, so we must start here or hereabouts.

We must then ask (we cannot ascertain; this is a fanciful exercise, after all) whether our disembodied person is himself occupying some spatio-temporal point. This might seem an odd question: how can he occupy some spatio-temporal point? He is, after all, disembodied. We must be tempted to say that he is in it because he sees things that are in it.

So where is he in the spatio-temporal realm? If the disembodied person sees what a normal observer sees then they look to that observer the way they look to our disembodied person. In other words, he must be at the centre of his visual field.

We cannot say that the disembodied person seeing things the way he does is a *consequence* of where he is: his being where he is *consists in* his seeing things the way he does.

Secondly, it is logically impossible to say that things look different to the disembodied person than the way they look to others. Indeed, how could the disembodied person *move* in order to get a better view? To give a sense to this idea it would have to be expressed in terms that are purely mental or introspective. So how do we present a mental sense to the notion of choosing to move to get a better view?

But *trying to get a better view* is the very notion we are trying to make sense of. It seems, then, that the notions we are trying to use are not simply introspective notions: they cannot supply what we need.

But if it makes sense to say that the disembodied person is, *merely by trying*, to be elsewhere then we would have to be able *a priori* to say this of an embodied person. But this we cannot do! Such a person would be regarded as a kind of superman.

Therefore, in trying to ascribe to a disembodied person an attempt to get a better view we need to endow him with powers we would not even ascribe to ourselves.

It might be objected that such a disembodied person might well be endowed with such powers. But we must remember that here we are trying to make *sense* of such ascriptions, not to engage in flights of fancy.

A disembodied person cannot, *ex hypothesi*, have perceptions of his own bodily states. But now we are back to the issue of the possibility of having *any* sensations which are not a perception of bodily states.

What of the ascription of agency to the disembodied person? To say that he has done something? For example, one asks: 'What is left over when we subtract the fact that the table rose from the fact that the spirit raised the table?' Here an analogy with the embodied person breaks down: whatever is 'left over' cannot be identical with the operations of embodied persons (say, putting his hands under the table to make it rise upward). As we have seen, the disembodied person must be perceived to raise it through some *mental* act. What else could the 'left over' consist in? So, the mental acts of the disembodied person and the physical acts of the embodied person are crude analogues. I say 'crude' of the differences: an embodied person must go through physical actions to raise the table; this option is denied our disembodied person.

We have proceeded, so far, on the unstated assumption that the disembodied person 'inhabits' the world we inhabit. How else could he have anything to perceive or to do? But what of the notion that those who survive death do so in *another* world? Of course, this other world can only be intelligible for us if we use the language of our world of things and persons to describe it: only if talk about it is intelligible can we understand the claim that the disembodied person might perceive or act in it. One difficulty here is that a disembodied person living in an alternate world is doomed to solipsism. The surviving disembodied person could perceive no other thing or person because those 'others' could have no perceptible characteristics.

A disembodied person, *ex hypothesi*, has no body. Let us set aside for the moment the vexed question of how it is possible to have memories without a brain. It is essential, in considering a memory-based foundation for disembodied existence, to be able to distinguish between one disembodied person and another. We clearly cannot say that Jones^a at T^1 and Jones^b at T^2 are identical because they shared the same body or, indeed, any physical characteristics. But if Jones^b at T^2 has memories shared with Jones^a at T^1 (but not those of Smith at T^1. Such a schizophrenic complication could be multiplied and makes any notion of identity incomprehensible) then we might have a starter.

Now memories are, of course, notoriously unreliable. For any degree of plausibility, the memory-thesis must refer to *good* memories; in other words, verifiable memories. *Remembers* functions a little like *knows*: if I know x, then x must be true. If I remember x, in the *good* memory sense, then x must be true. There is a weaker sense of *remembers* in which Smith merely *believes* that he remembers x in the strong sense. Here he remembers without it being necessary that what he remembers is true. Here we speak of mis-remembering.

For the memory-thesis to be successful it, obviously, must be memory in the *good* sense we are talking about. In other words, we are talking about occasions where someone remembers what happened *did in fact* happen. For this to be the case, some independent form of verification is necessary. In this sense, the memory-thesis is not an independent standard of identity.

But this means that without recourse to the bodily presence of the person at some past time, we are unable to understand what it would be like to determine that some event or action is, or is not, part of this person's past life. So, we would have no standard of identity to use of the disembodied person at all.

This is enough to put out of the question an intelligible concept of disembodied survival.

We must first address the semantic question of whether we can *understand* the notion of the existence of disembodied persons through time before we address the epistemological issue about whether we can *know* this is the case.

Both bodily identity and memory are criteria of personal identity. But are these the only means of identifying people? There is a host of physical ways identity might be established: primarily, I think, physical recognition including looking at a passport/driver's license, etc. But also: DNA sequencing, fingerprinting, blood tests, birthmarks or other distinguishing features.

The veracity of these methods of confirming identity depends on the truth that a person is a continuous physical organism, albeit one that changes over time.

We could add to this, somewhat more obliquely, similarities of character or skills; but these are secondary, more corroborative, tests than the ones mentioned above.

My contention will be that, although memory may be used as a criterion of personal identity, this depends in critical ways upon the existence of the bodily criterion of identity. Memory alone could not be a criterion of identity if in claiming to have had x's experience x actually also had x's physical features.

For us to accept memory-claims about a person's own past as true we need, as Penelhum argues:

'a) to recognize him throughout a contemporary period of time,

b) to have access to our own, or some third party's, records or recollections of the stretch of past personal history to which he lays claim, and

c) to identify the owners of these two with each other on the basis of considerations other than the content of the memory-claims themselves' (*op. cit.*).

The problem is that (a – c) are, in principle, unavailable if the memory-criterion stands alone without the bodily-criterion. As Penelhum concludes: 'Hence memory could not be the only standard of personal identity, since if it were it could not, paradoxically, be applied. It is, then, not an *independent* criterion' (*op. cit.*).

The idea that memory could be a sole identity-criterion is empty. It is due to the incoherence of the view that memories are self-authenticating which, clearly, they are not.

It might be objected that in establishing bodily criteria for identity-claims we are often dependent on memory-claims. And this is undoubtedly true. But, as I have shown, to establish memory-claims in the absence of bodily criteria is not possible.

Memory-claims are parasitic upon bodily-claims.

There is no parity of one with the other in that bodily-claims could be established quite straightforwardly in the absence of the memory-claims *of the person himself* and this shows there is no equivalent of dependence between bodily-claims and memory-claims.

Bodily identity is a necessary, as well as a sufficient, condition for the identity of persons. Any attempt to establish personal identity on memory-claims alone is doomed to failure. Strawson concurs (*Individuals – An Essay in Descriptive Metaphysics*, 1959):

'... we build up our single picture of the world, of particular things and events, untroubled by possibilities of massive reduplications, content, sometimes, with the roughest locations of the situations and objects we speak of, allowing agreed proper names to bear, without further explanation, an immense individuating load. This we do quite rationally, confident in a certain community of experience and sources of instruction. Yet it is a single picture which we build, a unified structure, in which we ourselves have a place, and in which every element is thought of as directly or indirectly related to every other; and the framework of the structure, the common, unifying system of relations is spatio-temporal. By means of identifying references, we fit other people's reports and stories, along with our own, into the single story about empirical reality; and this fitting together, this connexion, rests ultimately on relating the particulars which figure in the stories in the single spatio-temporal system which we ourselves occupy' or, more simply: '... the character of a person's *perceptual experience* is dependent on facts about his own body' and '... a necessary condition of states of consciousness being ascribed at all is that they should be ascribed to the *very same things* as certain corporeal characteristics, a certain physical situation &c.' (*op. cit.*).

But this now means that if personal identity claims are dependent on bodily criteria (including their parasitic subset of memory-claims) then the notion of establishing the possibility of a disembodied person becomes a chimera.

Does this mean that any attempt to formulate a notion of the disembodied person is impossible? The physical tests necessary to show personal identity also show that without their application there could be no reason for the concept of personal identity, and the removal in the doctrine of survival of the availability of tests entails the removal of the possibility of such a reason in the disembodied case, not merely the removal about chances of knowing whether this test or that is satisfied. There are good reasons, therefore, for rejecting the suggestion that we can render the identity of a disembodied person intelligible, since the subtraction of the body leaves the notion of genuine memory chronically incomplete.

Disembodied existence becomes incoherent. Now where does this leave the believer in *karma*/reincarnation? Is it possible that, in the absence of disembodied persons, sense can be made of the notion of *karma* enacted through reincarnation?

To talk of the 'owned' experiences of disembodied persons Jones[a] and Jones[b] at T^1 and T^2, it is necessary to assume the intelligibility of reference to their owners which, given the above, cannot be done.

Memory could not be the sole and independent criterion of personal identity, since this would undermine the distinction between true and false memory beliefs about one's past, a distinction which can only exist if there is some further content to the notion of the identity of the rememberer and the owner of the action or experience remembered. Since this further content seems to derive from the possession of a body, or at least to be absent when this possession is excluded, the notion of the persistence through time of a disembodied being, and of its identification with a pre-mortem being, does not seem intelligible.

I conclude that the notion of the soul, construed as a disembodied person, is radically confused. If that is so, then the notion of *karma*, within the context of *samsara*, is equally radically confused.

CHAPTER 3
Karma and the Soul

It might be thought that the incoherence of the notion of a disembodied person obviates all talk of the soul. This does not necessarily follow.

Reductionists contend that I am nothing but my cells, host to millions of bacteria and my functioning can be explained in terms of biochemistry. On the other hand, there is a long and venerable belief in the existence of the soul. The nature of the soul (in Greek: *psyche*) occupies a central position in Plato's philosophy. Plato was, of course, principally influenced by Socrates but his ideas can also be found in Orphism and in Pythagoreanism.

Plato's discussion of the soul begins in the *Phaedo* but is taken up in the *Phaedrus* where we have his statement of the nature of the soul as 'self-motion'. In the *Laws* he says: 'That nature whose definition is self-motion is identical with that which is called soul'. In the *Meno* (81aff), the soul is eternal, and death and life are only phases of its existence in some bodily state. Later, in the *Philebus* and the *Timaeus*, he says that soul is not just something that belongs to human life, but the human soul is to be thought of as part of the world soul itself (*kosmos*). We shall encounter a notion not unlike this later when I look at *Brahman*.

His argument about the nature of the soul as self-motion was criticized by Aristotle (in *De Anima*), who also puts forward an argument connected with the nature of motion to prove the existence of a first unmoved mover (which Aquinas later took to be God). For Socrates, the soul is primarily a moral and religious category, and the necessity of living a holy life is not demonstrated by showing that the soul is eternal. This is what Wittgenstein refers to: 'The temporal immortality of the human soul, that is to say, its eternal survival after death, is not only in no way guaranteed, but this assumption in the first place will not do for us what we always tried to make it do. Is a riddle solved by the fact that I survive for ever? Is this eternal life not as enigmatic as our present one?' (*Tractatus* 6.4312).

The possibility of the soul's survival of death is one of the main questions in the first part of the *Phaedo*, but with the introduction of the question of generation and decay, this question is not so much in evidence as Plato developed his later views about the soul, and the question of human immortality took on a different aspect.

Like the Gnostics after him, and doubtless under the influence of the Pythagoreans, Plato believes that the body is the prison house of the soul, and the life of the philosopher is meant to be one in which he strives to overcome those influences of the body which prevent the soul from living that life that is proper to it; he thinks that the philosopher needs to purify his life of the evil influences that result from life in the body. In the *Phaedo*, he describes this as *katharsis* (67c).

For Plato, human life must not be just an exchange of pleasures, pains and fears. It must be a search for wisdom and virtue. When it is the former, then it becomes impossible to care for the life of the soul. It is these things that prevent the soul from gaining its purity. But they are not external to the life of the soul and just a part of bodily life; otherwise, the prisoner would not be the chief assistant in his own imprisonment. Plato's view here is one that can be seen evident in many religions. It is found in Christianity in the saying of Jesus: 'Lay not up for yourselves treasures upon earth where moth and rust doth corrupt, and where thieves break through and steal; but lay up for yourselves treasures in heaven where neither moth nor rust doth corrupt and where thieves do not break through and steal' (*Matthew* 6.19 – 20).

Plato connects the view in the *Phaedo* with the mystery religions of his own time. He says: 'I fancy that those men who established the mysteries were not unenlightened, but in reality had a hidden meaning when they said long ago that whoever goes uninitiated and unsanctified to the other world will lie in the mire, but he who arrives there initiated and purified will dwell with the gods. For as they say in the mysteries, "the thyrsus bearers are many, but the mystics are few"'(69c). Compare also: 'Strait is the gate and narrow is the way that leads to life, and few there be who find it' (*Luke* 13.24).

It is this Platonic influence in caring for one's soul that is evident also in the Hindu and Buddhist scriptures we have examined and which we will encounter later in modern Hindu and Buddhist literature. Ultimately, in the *Lysis* and the *Symposium*, Plato argues that it is love that is unchanging and eternal and it is love that will purify the soul.

[*Excursus*: Philosophers these days, it seems, enjoy the benefits of a semi-bureaucratic enhancement of their status to the point where they might, on the one hand, set up a private practice as 'ethicist' and on the other hand, hope for an invitation from the Prime Minister to advise on ethical aspects of moral or other problems. This is, partly, because ours is a culture which no longer distinguishes clearly between wisdom and expertise.

We need to distinguish between philosophy, whether of morality or whatever, as a practice for the subject of a discipline, and philosophy as Socrates practised it. A subject is something of which there may be acknowledged mastery and the masters of the subject determine what is the state of play in it at a particular time. Physicists postulate quarks, literary critics expatiate on texts and media studies persons do something or other, I am sure.

Subjects wax and wane, and at the moment, we are lost without interminable discussion of AI.

A subject waxing, or indeed waning, must be judged to be so by masters of it properly exercising those qualities of mind which are internal to the concept of the mastery of the subject, and which, for example, distinguish masters from novices or laymen, or masters of a subject from those whose intellectual interests are not part of the subject.

'How should one live?' was a question that Socrates asked and for him philosophy was the search, if not the answer, to that question. The general feeling of unease that I have about these matters arises from the Socratic impulse that learning is not, as the Sophists thought, simply subject or teaching-based; *it is actually about the kind of life we lead.* And that is why such matters as honesty, integrity, beauty, truth and goodness – all of them indefinable yet all indispensable - must sit at the heart and form the causal nexus of what philosophers try to do.

Too often, critics join with Aristophanes' audience, laughing at his mirthless caricature of Socrates in *The Clouds*. I should lay my cards on the table: I think Socrates was right. Philosophy should be about how one should live; it is far broader than a mere concatenation subjects.

One cannot drive a wedge between oneself as an individual human being and oneself as a philosopher. For Socrates, philosophy was not, and could not, have been a subject in the sense in which we speak of it when we speak of students being initiated into a subject. For most of us, education is like that; being initiated into a subject; hence the frustration and the unease. Philosophy is about how one should live one's life.]

The main difficulty which Plato faced in the *Phaedo*, and failed to solve, was how the soul can be regarded as immortal unless it is unchanging in character, since the immortal and divine are unchanging. At least the Forms are unchanging and eternal, and always the same, but human life and the life of the human soul cannot be regarded so. The soul can change, and the nature of its life can change, and this fact is brought out, in part at least, in Plato's account of metempsychosis, which appears in other accounts of the life of the human soul (in the myths of the *Gorgias*, the *Republic*, *Phaedrus*, and in the account of the creation of the human soul in the *Timaeus*). The doctrine of metempsychosis, however, is a part of Plato's attempt to see the life of the human soul as something which meets judgement for its life in the body, and the kind of life which a human soul will live in another incarnation is determined by the kind of moral striving it is able to attain in any human life it might live. One of the important points, stressed in the *Phaedo*, is that the life of the true philosopher is one which enables him so to take care of his soul, that he may have a sure hope that after death he me may go to live with the gods and escape from the 'wheel of rebirth'. It is the philosopher who is regarded as able, if anyone is, to live the kind of life which makes this escape possible, for his life is characterized by a moral striving which will enable him to avoid the judgement that naturally comes the way of the human soul.

With regard to this, the doctrine of *anamnesis* (reminiscence) is important. For the soul does not remember what it has learnt in a previous life; it can either recollect more clearly or more dimly, and whether its remembrance is clear and pure depends on the purity of the life which it has itself achieved. It is not merely that *anamnesis* is meant to prove the pre-existence of the human soul before birth; it also, in a way, shows that the soul is of such a nature that it can recollect what it once knew. We might say: the soul is not immortal because it thinks and reasons, but rather that this activity itself, which is regarded as that which makes *anamnesis* possible, is conceivable only because the soul itself is immortal in nature, or, as the matter is put in the *Phaedo*, akin to the divine unchanging. So the soul conceived as pre-existing before its life in the body must have had a life of a specific nature; if it did not have this kind of life it could not have known the Forms.

As we have seen, the *Puggalavadins* expended much energy over the question of the soul and its nature. But given the venerable history of commentary upon the soul, from the *Vedas*, through Pythagoras and Plato, to the *Puggalavadins*, can we make any sense of this notion? Does it make sense to identify the soul with the disembodied person? If it does not, then, as we have seen above, the notion of the soul can make no sense. I contend it does not.

'The notion of the self is not the notion of an inner substance, necessarily private, whose existence and nature we must guess or infer from bodily behaviour which is but a pale reflection of the reality behind it. Persons are not mysterious entities that we never meet directly or have direct knowledge of' (*Death and Immortality*, D.Z. Phillips, 1970).

As I have argued elsewhere (*The Anatomy of Belief and Unbelief*, 2023), that if one can show that the possibility of having some kind of inner life depends on there being common activities in a common language, then any attempt to identify the essence of the self – mind, soul, spirit, call it what you will – with an inner substance divorced from such connections, can be shown to be radically confused.

Without this bodily continuity or, indeed, as we have seen, without the body, there can be no content whatever in the notion of personal identity; this is one reason why the Hindu doctrine of *samsara* is a *non*sense.

Phillips says: 'Talk about the soul... is not talk about some strange sort of "thing". On the contrary, it is a kind of talk bound up with certain moral or religious reflections a man may make on the life he is leading. Once this is recognized, once one ceases to think of the soul as a thing, as some kind of incorporeal substance, one can be brought to see that in certain contexts talk about the soul is a way of talking about human beings' (*op. cit.*).

I take it, therefore, that talk about the soul falls prey to the fate of talk about the disembodied person, at least as far as *karma* is concerned.

CHAPTER 4
Karma and Reincarnation

Pythagoras taught the doctrine of rebirth/transmigration, which he probably learned from contemporary Orphics. Xenophanes mocked him for pretending to recognize the voice of a departed friend in the howls of a beaten dog (fr. 7). Empedocles likewise refers to a man who could remember what happened ten or twenty generations before (fr. 129).

As early as Plato's (427 – 347 BC) *Apology*, we find Socrates suggesting some sort of life beyond death to his accusers (the *Apology* is the setting of Socrates' trial for impiety which may yield the death penalty). Socrates says that death must be either total annihilation, in which case it is an unbroken rest, or else a change to another world. And if it is true as reported that no one can there converse with the great men of past time, how unrewarding! To meet Homer, Hesiod, or the great heroes of the old days, especially those similarly condemned to death unjustly, would be worth dying for again and again.

In the *Meno*, Socrates suggests that men's souls are immortal and undergo an endless cycle of deaths and rebirths. In the course of these rebirths, men's souls have come to know all things both in this world and the other. Knowing, therefore, is not a matter of acquiring something new but, rather, a matter of recollecting something known but afterwards forgotten (*anamnesis*).

In his remarkably modern and prescient *De Anima*, Aristotle

(384-322 BC) contends, apparently for the first time, that the soul – not a separate entity somehow (attached) to the body – is, in fact, the actual development of the potentialities of life; it is the body's source of movement, the essence of the living body, and the purpose for which the body exists. Sensation is the process of receiving into oneself, by means of the sense organs, the forms of things.

The mind is that part of the soul by which the soul knows and thinks.

Lucretius (c.98 – 55 BC) tells us that the soul is composed of atoms; hence, at death, the soul dies with the body.

In what sense does the reincarnated person count as the same person as the deceased? The Buddhist critique of Hindu metaphysics centred on this issue and the questions of King Milinda argue that any determination of sameness is essentially arbitrary.

For Plato, most Christians, the theologians of the first millennium, Descartes, *et al* the soul was the essential immaterial part of a human, temporarily united with its body.

Metempsychosis is a doctrine of repeated incarnations of souls, with punishment and rewards for behaviour in previous lives.

Given that the notion of a disembodied person is incoherent, as we have seen, then how are we to make sense of the idea of reincarnation? It would seem that the only option left to us is that, as Jones[a] dies, he is reincarnated into the body of Jones[b] in some such way that disembodiment is not involved. The only option seemingly available to us is some kind of contemporaneous resurrection.

I say 'contemporaneous' because anything other than contemporaneity would entail a gap between the death of Jones[a] and the birth of Jones[b] and, for there to be continuity of existence, there must not be disembodied existence in the gap. But I have shown the notion of the disembodied person to be incoherent.

Although not unheard-of, it is most unusual for believers in *samsara* that a birth of a post-mortem person follows immediately upon the death of that person. For most, there is a gap between one incarnation and another. So, what is it that exists between these incarnations? The answer may be: 'nothing'. This answer has to be possible for the doctrine of reincarnation to be possible. Yet only if the intermediate state could be given any intelligible description could any set of circumstances *require* the doctrine.

Will resurrection fit the bill? Putting aside the illogicality of disembodied existence of the interim, can the apparent deficit be made up by the notion of resurrection?

Let us assume that at some unspecified time in the future there appears persons in bodies similar to ours. They cannot be the same: there has not been bodily continuity. They claim to be long since dead persons, returned to life, with memories to fit their pre-mortem state and a similar appearance. Could we identify the pre- and post-mortem bodies?

There is a problem, I think, with the notion that Smith is able to predict *his own* future resurrection existence. This is not as unusual as it may sound. Most believers in *karma/samsara* (as with many Christians) are happy to speak of their expectations as regards their future incarnations. I shall consider the implications of what can be *known*, as opposed to what can be predicted, in the chapter, *Karma and Logic*, below.

With the gap between the death of the one body and the appearance of the resurrection-body, all necessity for saying Jones' successor is Jones disappears, however possible it is. And it does not seem that Jones *need* concern himself with being his own successor unless that successor *has* to be identified with Jones. And without the continuity of the body, the identification does not *have* to be performed. Disembodied personal identity is the only way to account for the gap by having the person imagined as continuing between death and resurrection. But since this is incoherent, we are at a loss: the all-too-easy acceptance of the intelligibility of this (resurrection) doctrine of survival has depended in practice upon the assumption of bodiless continuance.

What do we say to those who expect to be resurrected? That they seem also to believe in the immediate disembodied state which is demonstrably absurd? Consider here that many Christians expect to be raised 'at the Last Trump' thus necessitating a gap between death and resurrection.

The identification of pre- and post-mortem bodies cannot be stated in the resurrection doctrine without presupposing that the owner of the earlier body and the owner of the latter body are the *same* person. Otherwise, the gap in time between the dissolution of the earlier body and the appearance of the later body make it quite easy to say that they are merely two similar bodies.

Peter Geach rejects the doctrine of reincarnation. In respect of the Lockean doctrine of memory-claims, he says: ' ... Locke's doctrine is quite indefensible. If a person is to remember truly what he did at an earlier date, it must already be true, before he turns his mind to the question of what happened then, that the person who did the deed is the same person as the person who is now to be reminded of the matter; it cannot possibly be the case that the memory makes the person remembering to be the same person as the doer of the remembered deed' (*God and the Soul*, 1969).

But worse than this, Locke's doctrine is 'morally repugnant': 'We ought not to need a Freud to tell us that some men very readily forget their past misdeeds; I do not see why the possessors of such a convenient memory should be held the less responsible for what they have done – the mere fact of their being so constituted is often a sign of a vicious character. And even if a man's oblivion of a past misdeed is in itself wholly inculpable, his responsibility for the deed need not be diminished; a man who drives recklessly ought not to be excused by others or himself because he has forgotten the whole affair owing to concussion in the eventual crash. Perhaps Locke would think that God will hold such a man excused on Judgment Day; but I see no reason to think that' (*op. cit.*).

Geach also rejects the mind/body dualism of Descartes in dismissing the notion of disembodied spirits. There are insurmountable epistemological problems: ' ... it is not a question of whether seeing is (sometimes) a private experience, but whether one can attach meaning to the verb "to see" by a private uncheckable performance; and this is what I maintain one cannot do to any word at all.'

More particularly, as far as survival after death is concerned: 'The possibility of life after death for Peter Geach appears to stand or fall with the possibility of there being once again a man identifiable as Peter Geach. The existence of a disembodied soul would not be a survival of the person Peter Geach; and even in such a truncated form, individual existence seems to require at least a persistent possibility of the soul's again entering into the make-up of a man who is identifiably Peter Geach'.

Geach is of the view, *pace* Locke, that identity is dependent on material continuity: 'We cannot rightly identify a man living "again" with a man who died unless *material* conditions of identity are fulfilled.'

Geach is left to conclude, having rejected the notion of disembodied spirits and that of reincarnation that the only possibility for survival after death is resurrection: 'If ... memory is not enough for personal identity; if a man's living again does involve some bodily as well as mental continuity with the man who lived formerly; then we might fairly call this new bodily life a resurrection. So the upshot of our whole argument is that unless a man comes to life by resurrection, he does not live again after death ... apart from the possibility of resurrection, it seems to me a mere illusion to have any hope for life after death' (*op. cit.*).

Geach, and his wife Elizabeth Anscombe, were practicing

Catholics; they believed in a hope of the resurrection of the dead; they believed this on the basis of the resurrection of Jesus and the promise of the resurrection to faithful believers. And yet ... the New Testament teaching on resurrection is muddled: it is not at all clear what resurrection meant in the New Testament. The teaching of St Paul was radically different to the presentation of the resurrection in the Gospels.

St Paul on the Resurrection

I wish to contend that, as a matter of fact, St Paul *did not* believe in a bodily resurrection.

I have argued fully elsewhere (*Faith and Belief*, 1994) that St Paul did not believe in a bodily resurrection. I will here simply summarize that argument: 1 *Corinthians* 15, in the New Testament, is the earliest recorded account of Jesus' resurrection. It was probably written in the spring of A.D. 57. It is a curious chapter, at almost complete odds with the Gospel stories which were written between about 70 and 100 A.D.

In fact, the account predates Paul having been 'passed on' to him (v. 3), the original probably dating to the early thirties, not long after Jesus' death. We can reasonably assume this in that the passage is redolent with Aramaisms, *hapax legomena*, early formulae, and non-Pauline language.

The Greek is almost certainly a translation from Aramaic. In the chapter, Paul lists all the post-resurrection appearances known to him. It is interesting that he goes on to say: 'And if Christ be not risen, then is our preaching vain, and your faith is also vain' (v. 14). The veracity of the Christian faith, for Paul, rests on the 'historical' reality of the resurrection. And nothing more is adduced to support the resurrection than a list of witnesses: 'Kephas' (the Aramaic for Peter), 'the twelve' (a *hapax legomenon* in Paul's writing), 'more than 500 of the brothers at the same time', 'James', and lastly, to Paul himself.

Interestingly, apart from the 'appearance' to Peter, not one of these 'appearances' is to be found in the Gospels, or indeed, elsewhere in the New Testament. The truth of the resurrection in the Gospels is adduced from the story of the empty tomb. In all of St Paul's writing, he does not once mention the empty tomb.

Paul adds his own name to the list of appearances; this is a reference to his own experience on the road to Damascus recounted in curiously incompatible tales in the book of *Acts of the Apostles* (9:1-9; 22:5-11; 26:12-18).

In these tales, Jesus' appearance to Paul is in a 'vision' (26:19) from the sky (26:13) and Paul does not differentiate his own vision of the risen Jesus from that of the other appearances he lists.

In 1 *Corinthians* 15, Paul uses the Greek word *egeiro* for 'resurrection'. It generally means 'waking up' or 'rising' (from sleep); it is also, interestingly, the same verb that is used to refer to Jesus' 'ascension' into heaven.

A more interesting word is the one that Paul uses for 'appeared to' (the witnesses): *horao*. There are lots of other everyday words for 'seeing' or 'appearing' in Greek but *horao* is not one of them. The particular form of the verb in 1 *Corinthians*, and elsewhere (*opthe*: third person middle deponent (passive) aorist with the dative), means 'to have a vision'; it is a standard part of the language of revelation.

Paul believed that all post-resurrection appearances of which he knew were in fact, heavenly visions occurring over a period of years. The 'risen' Jesus was in fact the ascended Jesus, appearing in visions from heaven.

In true gnostic fashion, St Paul did not believe in a bodily resurrection of Jesus. That is why he never mentions the empty tomb: he had never heard of such a thing!

Of course, this places Paul at odds with the orthodox tradition of a bodily resurrection, as represented by the Gospels (although Mark has no resurrection, just an empty tomb). The resurrection stories in the Gospels are corporealized to combat the increasing influence of both Gnosticism and Docetism. From the Gospels to Paul, we see the change from an eschatological into a soteriological characterization. More often than not, Christians read Paul's writing on the resurrection through the lens of the corporealized picture painted in the Gospels.

St Paul wrote over half the New Testament (although not all he is generally credited with having written) and while Jesus, whose message was purely eschatological, was Christianity's founder, Paul was its inventor, particularly in terms of the Christian theology arising from the New Testament. Paul changed Jesus' eschatological message into a soteriological one (cf. John Casey, *After Lives,* 2009): 'The influence of Paul's vision on what became Christian orthodoxy cannot be exaggerated. (Indeed, some have argued that Paul was the true creator of Christianity, the religion that claimed to have superseded Judaism and abrogated the Law of Moses, the religion that turned Jesus the Jew into Jesus the Christian.)'

There can be little doubt that Paul perceived the resurrected Jesus, and also as we gather from the rest of his writings, all resurrected persons, as disembodied persons. Insofar as that is the case, then what I have argued above, in chapter 2 concerning disembodied persons, can be seen to apply, *mutatis mutandis,* to the notion of resurrection.

We have seen that reincarnation, construed in terms of the disembodied person, is incoherent. I have also argued that the only possible defensible setting for reincarnation must be construed as a series of resurrections. I have now shown that resurrection, at least as understood by the inventor of Christianity, was conceived in terms of disembodied persons. It would appear that, either way, the believer in reincarnation and/or in resurrection holds to a doctrine which is incoherent. I shall now argue that it is also illogical.

CHAPTER 5
Karma and Logic

In Graham Greene's short story, *A Shocking Accident*, we are told the tale of Jerome, a young boarding school boy, who is called into his Housemaster's office to be told that his father (whom Jerome suspected was a gunrunner or a member of the British Secret Service) has been killed in Naples. Jerome assumes that his father has been killed in some clandestine operation but, it transpires, that he was, in fact, killed by a falling pig: 'Your father was walking along a street in Naples when a pig fell on him. A shocking accident. Apparently in the poorer quarters of Naples they keep pigs on the back balconies. This one was on the fifth floor. It had grown too fat. The balcony broke. The pig fell on your father.'

Jerome finds himself wondering what happened to the pig.

In the following, I have adapted the schemata found in Nelson Pike's *God and Timelessness* (1970). Using our model of Graham Greene's story *A Shocking Accident*, and adapting Pike's schemata, consider the following:

Last Saturday afternoon, Jerome's father (JF) died when a pig fell on his head (instantiate any alternative/variable you like to maintain the argument *salva veritate*). Let us assume that the individual whose name is now JF, but in some previous life was Smith, is in fact the same person, reincarnated into a new body (having, if need be, undergone subsequent incarnations during the interim). It follows (let us say), that 800 years (any given time) prior to Saturday, Smith had murdered his aunt Fanny because he disliked her cooking and knew, because of this action, that unpleasant retribution would be affected because of his bad *karma*. From this we can conclude that at the time of the action (Saturday) JF was not able to refrain from being killed by a falling pig; or, to put it another way (and this is most important), the pig was not able to refrain from falling on JF. This was because the retribution was the result of Smith's bad *karma* which resulted from killing aunt Fanny. The causal efficacy of the first act determined the second. There was no way that JF could have avoided the retribution because of Smith's previous action.

Let us see if we can get a little clearer about the details.

Begin with the setting just described: JF is killed by a falling pig on Saturday and Smith believes 800 years earlier that JF (previously Smith) will be punished at some given future date (in this case 800 years in the future). The most obvious conclusion would seem to be that at the time of the action, JF was able to perform some other action (running like hell) and thereby save himself from the falling pig, the performance of which would have rendered Smith's belief false. But the doctrine of *karma* is causally efficacious in that B always follows A and it is logically impossible that JF can escape retribution. Thus, on Saturday, JF was not able to act in such a way as to render false the doctrine of *karma* expressed by Smith and effected 800 years earlier. To suppose that he was so able to act at the time of action, would be to suppose that he was able to do something with a conceptually incoherent description, viz. something that would render false the doctrine which is causally efficacious.

Hence, given that Smith believed 800 years ago that an inescapable action of retribution would be affected on him (JF), later (800 years, last Saturday) – which follows from the fact that JF was hit by a falling pig on Saturday plus the supposition that *karma* is a causal retribution system which necessarily brings about retributive effects and that this could be known by the actor prior to the retribution taking place – if we were to assign JF the power on Saturday to escape the falling pig, we must not describe that power as the ability so to act as to render a karmic causal relation false.

It might be objected that it is nonsense to believe that JF's being killed by a falling pig is the only way in which the karmic causal relation might be affected. The retribution may have been brought about in some other form of painfulness/unpleasantness (say, as a 'lower' rebirth) and at some other time (an earlier/later reincarnation).

But if one allows that JF can escape this karmic catastrophe last Saturday, then there is no logical impossibility in a man's escaping each and every possible karmic cataclysm that may come upon him, therefore nullifying the efficacy of karmic causality, which for the purposes of the example we are assuming is the case.

How then might we describe such a power (to escape the falling pig) vis-à-vis Smith's knowledge of the causal efficacy of *karma*? So far as I can see, there are only two alternatives: first, we might try describing it as the power to act such that Smith believed otherwise than he did 800 years earlier; and, secondly, we might try describing it as the power so to act that Smith (who by hypothesis existed 800 years earlier) did not exist and maintain a karmic belief 800 years ago. This last would be the power so to act that any individual who lived 800 years ago and believed that karmic retribution would be affected on JF (himself) in the future (800 years), (one of which was, by hypothesis Smith) would hold a false belief and thus would render *karma* invalid. Any individual holding such a false belief could not be right about *karma* and therefore, must be incorrect (given our assumptions so far).

However, neither of these alternatives can be accepted. As regards the first, let us agree that had JF actually escaped the falling pig on Saturday, (or had the efficacy of *karma* not been made manifest at any future time) then Smith would have believed otherwise than he did believe 800 years earlier: this follows from the fact that karmic retribution necessarily follows a bad deed and that this can be known by anyone (Smith) plus the assumption that if a causal law can be known at a given moment (T^1 – 800 years earlier) and is known by someone (Smith) who believes *p* (that karmic retribution will follow) at T^1. But this observation takes no account of the facts working in the case before us. JF was *in fact* killed by a falling pig on Saturday. Smith did *in fact* believe 800 years earlier that karmic retribution would follow: although obviously not in this particular way. It is, after all, unusual to be killed by a falling pig (except maybe in Naples in fiction).

On Saturday, JF did not have the power to escape the falling pig, the performance of which would require that Smith did not believe as he did in fact believe so long ago. By the time Saturday got here, Smith's belief was tucked away 800 years in the past. Nothing that JF was able to do on Saturday could have had the slightest bearing on whether Smith held a certain belief 800 years earlier. For similar reasons, the last of the alternatives mentioned cannot be accepted either. If Smith (a knowing person) existed 800 years earlier, we cannot assign JF the power on Saturday to perform an act, the description of which would entail that Smith did not exist 800 years ago.

We are now ready for the conclusion: given that JF was killed by the falling pig on Saturday and given that Smith (JF^1) existed and maintained a knowledge which had set in causal motion a certain later retributive effect (by killing aunt Fanny), it seems to follow that JF did not have the power on Saturday to escape the falling pig. The upshot is that JF's action ('fate') can be regarded as determined, or, that JF did not have the power or ability to do anything other than to be killed by the falling pig. This would lend credence to the idea of a causal relation between certain karmic acts and their retribution, in terms of logical viability. JF's action was not voluntary.

Since the argument just presented was rather complex, perhaps the following schematic representation may be of some use:

1. 'If *karma* is causally effective and is in operation at T^1' entails 'if JF does A at T^2, then his action is the effect of a previous karmic cause which can be known by JF (Smith) at T^1'.
2. If *karma* is (essentially) to be causally efficacious, then, '*karma* demonstrates p' entails 'p'.
3. It is not within one's power to act at a given time so that both p and not p are true.
4. It is not within one's power at a given time so to act that something believed by an individual at a time prior to the given time was not believed by that individual at the prior time.
5. It is not within one's power to act at a given time that an individual existing at a prior time did not exist at that prior time.
6. If Smith believes at T^1 that JF does A at T^2, then if it is within JF's power at T^2 to refrain from doing A then either:

a) it is within JF's power at T^2 to act, so that Smith believed p at T^1 and p was false; or

b) it was within JF's power at T^2 to act so that Smith did not believe as he did at T^1; or

c) it was within JF's power so to act at T^2 so that Smith did not exist at T^1.

7. If *karma* is causally efficacious and can be known by individuals, then the first alternative in the consequent line of (6a) is false (from points 2 and 3).
8. The second alternative of the consequent of line (6b) is false (from point 4).
9. The third alternative of the consequent line of (6c) is false (from point 5).
10. Therefore: if *karma* is (essentially) a causally efficacious

system which can be known and it is believed by Smith at T^1 that JF does A at T^2 (these are variables – whatever action or time you like) then it was not within JF's power at T^2 to refrain from doing A (from points 6 and 7-9).

11. Therefore: if *karma* is (essentially) a causally efficacious system which can be known and if it is believed by Smith at T^1 that JF does A at T^2, it was not within JF's power at T^2 to refrain from doing A (from points 10 and 1).

There are many assumptions implicit in the argument which I shall endeavour to unpack:

i) '*karma* is causally efficacious' is essential or a necessary statement (the proposition should be read as having a hypothetical form);

ii) if *karma* is causally efficacious then '*karma* demonstrates', entails '*p*'. If karmic actions can be known by a given individual then if '*x* believes *p*', entails '*p*' and '*q*' (the retribution);

iii) if '*p* is karmic' entails '*q*', it is not the case that 'not *q*' i.e. *karma* will present no identifiable karmic actions which do not produce effect '*q*';

iv) causality is an essential property of *karma*. A statement of the form 'if A is a karmic action, then A is causal' is a necessary truth, if it is true at all;

v) that there is an afterlife, or alternatively, that transmigration and *samsara* are true;

vi) that any individual (or at least certain individuals) who lived that T^1 can be identified as that same individual at T^2;

vii) that specific actions (A at T^2) can be identified as retribution for previous actions at T^1.

Now in the foregoing argument, points (1) and (2) are direct consequences of some of these assumptions – in particular, assumptions i, ii, iii, v, vi, vii. Points (3), (4) and (5) express what I take to be part of the concept of ability or power as it applies when speaking of human beings. Point (6) is offered as a necessary truth. If JF is given the ability to refrain from action A then his power must be described in one of the ways listed in the consequence of (6). There are no other alternatives.

Item (11), when generalized for all agents and actions, seems to be a minimum condition for the application of the phrase 'voluntary action', and yields the conclusion that if *karma* is causally efficacious after T^1 no human action is voluntary.

Of course, nothing important in the argument turns on our selection of the name Smith or on the selection of a particular time (T^1, 800 years ago) as a point of reference; this seems to warrant the conclusion: if *karma* is a causal operation and is efficacious, no karmic action performed is voluntary.

Now, how can there be any morality in retribution for involuntarily performed actions? Of course there can't!

The doctrine of *karma* entails thorough-going determinism.

Several objections might be offered here. It may be objected that it is not the case that it is believed that specific unpleasant acts (e.g. being killed by a falling pig) are the form of retribution affected by earlier specific karmic acts. It might be objected that the form of retribution normally takes the effect of rebirth into a 'hell' or 'lower' form of existence in the next life, say, as a worm, or as a dog, or even as a worm in the belly of a dog (as is claimed in the K.U. 1.2).

All that need be noted here is that *it is the case* that specific individual and complex, pleasant/unpleasant acts *are* seen as a result of good/bad *karma*. As we shall see later, Sadhguru claims that 'you still have your great-grandmother's arthritic knee'. This type of objection also misunderstands the nature of the quantified example. One may substitute 'the accumulation of good/bad *karma*' for the specific 'killed aunt Fanny' or 'was killed by a falling pig' as only instantiations for which a great range of acts may be substituted. It might also be objected that any given pleasant/unpleasant act may be explained in terms of *karma* as the result of any previous deed/misdeed of *any* given person and *any* previous time.

We are now in a position to deal more fully with the problems raised by free will/determinism in our model. The first problem is that which was alluded to earlier: that if Smith exists at T^1 he can only know what is true at T^1. Seeing that an action at T^2 has not occurred at T^1 it is neither true nor false, therefore unknowable. This argument, however, makes no mention of the causes of human action. It turns, instead, on the notion of its being true 800 years ago (i.e. for Smith to know at T^1 that JF receives retribution at T^2, it must be true at T^1 that JF receives retribution T^2). JF was not able to escape retribution at T^2. To suppose that he was, would be to suppose that on Saturday, JF was able to act in such a way as to render false a proposition that was already true 800 years earlier.

Following this type of reasoning, in order to force Smith to know at T^1 that JF receives retribution at T^2, it must be true at T^1 that JF receives retribution at T^2. Given the argument just sketched, if it is true at T^1 that JF receives retribution at T^2, then it is not within JF's power at T^2 to escape retribution. If we put these two arguments together it will follow that the doctrine of *karma*, understood in this way, entails thorough determinism. It does so by means of an intermediate thesis, specifically, the claim that propositions describing human actions are true at times prior to the times the actions are performed. A way to escape such a deterministic conclusion is to deny this intermediate thesis. Thus, in reference, say, to our example, proponents of such an argument solve the problem by denying points (1) and (2) and stating simply that such things are unknowable: the fact that a man acts in a certain way at a certain time is not knowable prior to the time of the action. No one could know it; the presupposition of foreknowledge is absent. Such a conclusion denies any human foreknowledge whatsoever (*reductio ad absurdum*).

Surely in any adequate analysis of 'foreknowledge' and 'voluntary action' one must allow that at least in some cases one can have knowledge of how another will 'voluntarily' act in the future. The problem here is that action A mentioned in the original statement is dated in the original statement. If one then dates the truth-value of the statement as a whole, it cannot be restated in accordance with the pattern such as: I state: 'JF does A at T^2'. You reply: 'That is true at T^1'. What would this mean? That JF does A at T^2? Surely not! The statement resulting assigns two incompatible dates to the action mentioned. How then can the statement be understood?

It might be that this is to be understood as affirming that if one guessed, asserted, thought, etc. at T^1 that JF does A at T^2, his guess, assertion, thought, etc. would be right (cf. G. Ryle, 'It was to be', *Dilemmas*, 1954). Or it might be read as to affirm that at T^1 there was sufficient evidence or grounds upon which a well-based prediction that JF does A at T^2 could be made (cf. R. Gale, 'Endorsing Predications', *Phil. Review*, 1961). We have already seen though in the story of the fortuneteller that all foreknowledge, at least, does not presuppose evidence or grounds.

I can see no reason why Smith's foreknowledge *must* be true at T^1 if Smith is to know at T^1 that JF does A at T^2 (cf. R. Albritton's, 'Present Truth & Future Contingency', *Phil. Review*, 1957).

Now as to the next problem, at the conclusion of the model it was decided that: 'It was not with in JF's power to refrain from doing A'. Now, when dealing with ordinary human agents, it is perfectly possible to know how another is going to act in advance of the action and even how they will freely choose to act. I know my wife would always order white wine at a restaurant, but she does so freely in spite of my 'foreknowledge'. But on the set of assumptions and the concluding schematic presentation of our model, it was concluded that JF was not free; it was concluded that 'if Smith believed at T^1 that JF does A at T^2' entails 'JF was not free to do otherwise'. If this was otherwise, we could conclude that the karmic relation did not hold and would therefore be false, which, *given the assumptions*, was absurd. There, the first entailed determinism, but the second regarding my wife's actions did not. Wherein lies the difference? The difference lies in the fact that both examples entail two contingent facts but one relies on an additional contingency. In both cases, x believes (knows) that y does A at T^2. This is simply to say that in both cases x *correctly* believed that y does A at T^2. In the last case, my wife was able to refrain from doing A (ordering white wine) thus rendering my belief false.

So, in both cases we are supposing that x believes at T^1 that y does A at T^2. Therefore, what appears to be a single contingency involves two contingencies, viz. that x held a certain belief at T^1 *and* that that belief was true. This additional contingency was understandable in the second example but not quite so in the first. Smith could not have been wrong about JF as I could have been wrong about my wife, because this was given in the assumptions (i) - (vii). It is quite possible, however, that Smith might have interpreted *karma* wrongly, JF might wrongly have been identified as Smith^x, etc. This shows that although human action could make the example almost impossible to demonstrate (even given all the assumptions listed), it is not human action that is being queried in the first example (as it is in the second); *it is the law of karma*. In the former case (but not in the latter), y was not able to refrain from A at T^2. Much of this, however, revolves around the nature of *karma* itself, as is evident in the debate of the *Kathavatthu*.

The doctrine of *karma* as a causal determinant is consistent within the structure of a system of doctrines, but derives its consistency only in the context of and from these related doctrines, notably those of *samsara* and rebirth.

For *karma* to be demonstrable, certain very difficult assumptions need to be shown. But isn't all religion based on certain non-empirical 'givens'? The models are important and acceptable to the believer, not only the demonstration. Although widely accepted, the doctrine places a great anxiety on the believer who becomes the causal nexus of his own destiny within a wider frame of causality known as *karma*.

We can safely conclude, therefore, that there is no such thing as *karma*. Even if there were, it would be thoroughly immoral, given that it entails the notion that it is just to punish the innocent for actions which are determined. The notion is not only fanciful but incoherent, not least of which because identity over time depends on identifiable bodily continuity.

CHAPTER 6
Karma and God

In the Christian tradition at least, God is believed to be personal but incorporeal. If the idea of the disembodied person is logically incoherent, then must we not say that the same challenge applies, *mutatis mutandis*, to God or the Gods?

God loves us, so Christianity informs us, by his *actions* (especially in the incarnation of Jesus Christ). But how are we to understand the notion of divine agency? Particularly as God does not have a body (except on the ceiling of the Sistine chapel!).

Karma and the Problem of Evil

As I write, storm Daniel has swept the coast of Libya killing thousands of people. Many of those interviewed, even in speaking of dead family members, have said this is an act of God. What is the difference between saying of some natural event (or even of some event in human history) that it is also an act of God?

The problem of evil, in the context of *karma*, has a long tradition in Indian religion. Adi Sankara in *Brahma Sutra bhasya* from the eighth century, notes that God cannot reasonably be the cause of the world because of the existence of evil and suffering. Such ruminations can also be found in the *Mahabharata*: one theory is that everything is ordained by God; alternatively, *karma* accounts for the evil/suffering in the world, and, finally, that it's all down to chance (*yadrccha*). In this epic, Lord Krishna debates the problem from all three perspectives but, in the end, it offers no conclusive answer.

Swinburne (see, e.g., *Faith and Reason*, 1981, see also my chapter 'Swinburne on Miracles' in *Faith and Belief – A Philosophical Approach*, 1994) attempts to say that these acts of God are discernible in patterns which we might expect of a living God. But such a suggestion will not help to distinguish this claim that these events are acts of God from the mere claim that the world is improving, or other such platitudes. It also faces the problem of morally disastrous consequences.

As we have seen, Weber sees the doctrine of *karma* as the perfect antidote to the question of a theodicy (i.e. attempts to vindicate divine providence in the face of the existence of evil). It is doubtless for this reason that theodicy has much exercised Christians in a way that it has not bothered Hindus and others.

The Problem of Evil, from Epicurus via Philo of Alexandria to today, has usually been presented in more or less the same way. We are generally offered three, sometimes more, propositions:

1) God is omnipotent

2) God is good/loving

3) evil/suffering exists

and the suggestion is that these three propositions, although all believed by many religious believers to be true, are mutually contradictory. These are held to be contradictory because, 'if God exists, then being omniscient, he knows under what circumstances evil will occur, if he does not act; and being omnipotent he is able to prevent its occurrence. Hence, being perfectly good, he will prevent its occurrence and so evil will not exist' (Swinburne, *op. cit.*).

Plantinga sees the problem in much the same kind of way:

'... Five propositions... essential to traditional theism: a) that God exists, b) that God is omnipotent, c) that God is omniscient,

d) that God is wholly good, and e) that evil exists... Each of these propositions is indeed an essential feature of orthodox theism. And it is just these five propositions whose conjunction is said... to be self-contradictory' ('The Free Will Defence', *The Philosophy of Religion*, ed., B. Mitchell, 1971). These writers are not unrepresentative of the vast number of philosophers who see, and try to solve, the problem in these terms.

The usual way to tackle the problem is to argue that it does not necessarily follow that an omnipotent being will want to prevent all evil/suffering, because the existence of evil/suffering is a necessary concomitant of a world in which free beings freely choose to worship the Creator such as the one envisaged in the original problem, and the latter state of affairs is more desirable than the one in which there are no free beings:

'A world containing creatures who freely perform both good and evil actions – and do more good than evil – is more valuable than a world containing quasi-automata who always do what is right because they are unable to do otherwise. Now God can create free creatures, but he cannot causally or otherwise determine them to do only what is right; for if he does so they do not do what is right *freely*. To create creatures capable of moral good, therefore, he must create creatures capable of moral evil; but he cannot create the possibility of moral evil and at the same time prohibit its actuality. And as it turned out, some of the free creatures God created exercise their freedom to do what is wrong: hence moral evil. The fact that free creatures sometimes err however, in no way tells against God's omnipotence or against his goodness; for he could forestall the occurrence of moral evil only by removing the possibility of moral good' (Plantinga, *op. cit.*).

I want to suggest, however, that this way of presenting the problem not only clouds the real issues involved but also creates more of a problem than it solves. I shall question some fundamental assumptions involved in the presentation of the problem in this way and attempt to show that, not only do they render the attempted solutions empty, but show that, if there is a problem of evil, it is not of the sort hitherto assumed to be the case.

The particular assumption with which I'm primarily concerned is the way in which the presentation of the argument, as I have outlined it, entails certain notions of the way God has, or has failed, to act.

Let us consider the case of a small child suffering from an incurable disease. This, on the face of it, appears to be a prime example of the sort of evil that God is said to be responsible for not preventing (arch-'anti-theodicists' such as Antony Flew and Dostoevsky's Ivan Karamazov always appeal to such cases, no doubt because of their emotive force). But what would it be for God actually to prevent such an evil? I can think of the following possible candidates for the class of events that might constitute God's prevention of the evil:

a) A direct and miraculous intervention whereby the laws of nature are suspended or contravened and the child is, as a result, healed.

b) The apparently natural remission of the disease which is construed as God's action.

There is no *logical* contradiction in either notion, but the question I want to consider here is just what sense can be made of them (see my 'Miracles and Violations', *International Journal for Philosophy of Religion*, 1982, and 'Miracles and Coincidences', *Sophia*, 1983).

What sense can be made of (a) in the context of the story we are considering? What would a miraculous intervention be in this instance? We are obviously not meant to construe God's intervention as akin to that of an invisible surgeon with infinite medical knowledge and powers, mending torn sinews, restoring damaged cells, in such a way that the human eye cannot see. Or are we? Does God really intervene in this fashion? Apart from the fact that I can make no sense of this sort of 'intervention' I can see other problems with it: in such a notion we seem to assume that God has good reasons for intervening in some cases but not in others. Suppose that the child in our example dies of this disease. Are we then to assume that God had good reasons for allowing the child to die? Or, if you like, to die in pain and suffering? Well... what are the reasons? To impugn God's character by laying moral blame on him is to misconstrue the nature of God in the first place. It involves a question of whether it is logically conceivable that God is malicious. But the problem here, it seems to me, is not whether or not God has reasons to intervene in one case rather than another but what sense it makes to lay blame on God. Professor Flew puts the challenge thus:

'Now it often seems to people who are not religious as if there was no conceivable event or series of events the occurrence of which would be admitted by sophisticated religious people to be sufficient reason for conceding "there wasn't a God after all" or "God does not really love us then". Someone tells us that God loves us as a father loves his children. We are reassured. But then we see a child dying of inoperable cancer of the throat. His earthly father is driven frantic in his efforts to help, but his heavenly father reveals no obvious sign of concern. Some qualification is made – God's love is "not merely human love" or it is "an inscrutable love", perhaps – and we realize that such sufferings are quite compatible with the truth of the assertion that "God loves us as a father (but, of course...)". We are reassured again. But then perhaps we ask: what is this assurance of God's (appropriately qualified) love worth, what is this apparent guarantee really a guarantee against? Just what would have to happen not merely (morally and wrongly) to tempt us also (logically and rightly) to entitle us to say "God does not love us" or even "God does not exist"? I therefore put ... the simple central question, "what would have to occur or to have occurred to constitute for you a disproof of the love of, or the existence of, God?" ('Theology and Falsification', *New Essays in Philosophical Theology*, 1955).

But what is Flew asking for here? Reasons for evil or suffering? Those who are willing to answer questions such as this usually point to God's design and argue that, although we cannot be sure at present, present suffering will be explained in relation to this design when we are in a better position to appreciate that design (usually when we had dead!). This answer is unhelpful. It places responsibility for evil/suffering squarely in God's lap – so to speak. It is the former in that the only chance one is given for being able to understand what circumstances mitigate our present malaise is in the hereafter; which could mean we will never find ourselves in such a position where we will be able to understand the problem. Although such answers may be creditable in that, in one sense at least, they directly attempt to answer the question, they are malicious in that we are left with the inescapable conclusion that the child's suffering is part of a premeditated plan; a plan designed by God before the world began. And we can surely do no other than agree with Ivan Karamazov that if this is the price for truth (free will, goodness, call it what you will) then the price is far too high! God's character is successfully impugned; he ceases to be worthy of worship. But answering the question in this fashion only goes to show that it is the wrong kind of question in the first place. The theist should not place himself in a position where he is forced to lay blame at someone's door.

Why should we feel we have to explain the cause of the cancer the child is suffering in terms of anything other than a medical explanation? We no longer have to explain the actions of the waves in terms of Poseidon's anger; we have a perfectly adequate explanation in terms of currents, tides, the earth's relation to the moon, etc. Need we look for anything more? Why then do we feel the need to look beyond red-and-white corpuscles, tumors, damaged cells and the like to explain the cause of cancer? *Cancer carries within itself the cause of its existence.* Why, in this latter case, we should need to look beyond this to see it as an effect of some antecedently devised plan preordained by God (especially considering that we see no need to do this in the former case of the waves) is a great mystery to me.

I am led by these considerations to conclude that (a), which construes God's intervention as somehow direct and miraculous, not only makes very little sense as a notion of the action of God, it leads to the point where its protagonists find themselves embroiled in arguments about how to mitigate God from the blame for these very interventions they are trying to explain. Not only is this notion of blame for evil/suffering one which makes little sense, it is also one with morally disastrous consequences for God.

Those who wish to follow path (b) also encounter difficulties. Suppose that, as I suggested in (b) above, the child recovers against all odds. Does it make sense here to say that God intervened? Yes, in a way it does. There is nothing inherently contradictory in construing this as an act of God. But the *philosophical* problem here is what it *means* to say God has healed the child. In addition to facing the difficulty of showing why God chose to save this child and not others, it also raises the problem of showing how this particular event qualifies as an act of God. What is it for *this* event to have religious significance? It might be suggested that an event such as this is consistent with the supposed nature of the Deity, or, alternatively, that it occurs in a context which is specifically religious. How then can the believer show that the nature of God, with which these events are thought to be consistent, has been revealed? The revelation cannot easily be said to issue itself in like events, for that would end in a quandary of circularity: the religious significance of other events cannot be adduced in support of event *x* to show that *x* is consistent with the nature of God because it is precisely the religious significance of *any* event that is in question here. But at what point in the 'healing' does it make sense to say 'God did this' or 'unless God did things this way we would not have had the resultant healing'?

In a case such as the one we have been considering, God's activity is apparent because the event excites us, or causes wonder, or because the event is inexplicable in medical terms. However, inasmuch as all events may, on the theistic conception of things, be related to the divine providence, then all events may, in one way or another, be said to be the action of God; and insofar as this may excite, amaze, or prove inexplicable, then all acts may be called the action of God.

Recent attempts in theology to escape the action of God as apparently arbitrary and sporadic interventions in the history of the world have resulted in the idea that everything is an act of God. But if God's action is applicable to every class of events and, in some cases, to every *thing*, then the words 'God's action' seem to me to have lost any substantive content either as that which excites wonder, on the one hand, or as individual enough to be construed as the separate class of acts, called 'God's acts', on the other. Consider:

    1. Everything is a miracle, and
    2. Miracles excite wonder, then, (from (1) and (2))
    3. Everything excites wonder.

So, by substitution in (1) above,

    4. That which excites wonder excites wonder.

This does not seem to me to be a very significant tautology, hence my claim that 'everything is a miracle' lacks substantive content. Nor is it made any more substantive by saying, as theists do, that everything that happens is due to the 'action of God' because if,

5. Everything that happens is due to the action of God and this excites wonder (from (3) above),

6. Then we are back with (1) and (2) above (which will yield the same conclusion), in that 'everything that happens is due to the action of God' is elliptical for saying that 'everything is a miracle'. Unless, that is, there are certain actions of God which are not miracles and which do not, as such, excite wonder. But once we arrive at this conclusion we are talking about a different view of miracles to the one I have outlined above.

If events admit of natural or historical explanation yet are called 'miracles' or 'acts of God' then their only claim to fame as a class of events which are different from others will be that they are wondrous, or exciting, or coincidental. Such an arbitrary criterion for the evaluation of an event to be subsumed under such a class leaves the door wide open to all kinds of events very vaguely construed as such. For example, how would one determine which events are wondrous, exciting, coincidental *enough* to qualify as acts of God? Nor can it be sustained, as we shall see below, that the significance of an event called 'miraculous' or 'act of God' is so because of the relation it bears to human needs, hopes, and fears. The general relation of so many events, both wondrous and not so wondrous, to so many human aspirations and needs (which may be called luck, fate, coincidence, etc.) would suggest that there are other criteria by which an event is construed as an act of God.

So then, we find that on (b), claims to identify God's activity have either ended up as vacuous or meaningless. At the other extreme, if God's activity is indistinguishable from the daily vicissitudes of life, then the theist is going to have a hard time showing that, like Schleiermacher and Spinoza before him, he is not embracing some form of pantheism.

My conclusion then is that the problem of evil is only a problem if it is construed in such a way that entails a notion of God's power and goodness which is unworkable. The solution involves a radical restructuring of the idea of God's power and goodness but not one, I suggest, which is inconsistent with the idea of God's power and goodness found in the biblical paradigms of faith.

Consider the story of Job. Job suffers the most tragic of evils and, if anyone can be, he should be in a position to blame God for his non-intervention. That is, if he were to attribute goodness to God by an intervention in the course of events in his life. Yet this is not Job's reaction. He says: '... The Lord gave, and the Lord hath taken away; blessed be the name of the Lord' (1.21). This shows that for Job the notion of God's goodness and power is not dependent on the way things have happened to him. In other words, he does not utilize the course of events as an explanatory hypothesis for God's existence.

Swinburne says: 'It is not logically possible to create humanly free agents such that necessarily they do not do moral evil actions' ('The Problem of Evil' in S.C. Brown, *Reason and Religion*, 1977). But surely disdain of evil could be taught, as most often it is, by hypothetical inference without actual evils taking place? Swinburne's 'logically' here is hardly that.

Generosity, kindness, loyalty, truth, etc., all get their identity in a world where meanness, cruelty, disloyalty and lies are also possible. We see the importance of virtues, not in the face of apparent or possible evils, but in the face of actual evils.

When we think we ought to be generous, is it in the face of apparent need or real need? How could we know the difference?

These kinds of issues come about in the so-called 'free will defence'. In this, God does not create a world where man always does right because then they would not be morally free. But just what can it mean to say that God sees to it, or ensures, that men always do what is right? When it comes to the development of human character, I can make no sense of what such 'ensuring' or 'seeing to' amounts to.

I have no problem with saying that some things happen and that these can be character-forming. Some people, in the face of torture, collapse; others show a fortitude they never knew they had. But how is strength in the face of torture taken up into the rest of a person's life? How do we speak of God 'seeing to it' or 'ensuring' such an outcome in this context? What on earth would it mean to say that such 'ensuring' can be detected here? My difficulty is to find a discernible difference in human affairs which could confirm or refute these speculations about God's 'seeing to it'.

So what does it mean to suggest that God 'ensures' that human characters are of such and such a kind? Measures taken by parents may influence the development of their children, sometimes in ways they hope for. But who is able to say, sensibly, 'I saw to it, or ensured, that my child's character developed thus and so?' So much is outside the control of the agent.

Not only need evil *not* occasion goodness, but goodness itself may occasion evil. The depth of a man's love may lead him to kill his wife's lover or to be destroyed when the object of his love is lost to him. A man whose love was mediocre would not have done either of these things. Love has as much to do with the terrible as with the wonderful. The presence of goodness in some may be the cause of hatred in others.

The theodicist, including Swinburne, feels he has to answer the question why his God does not intervene in circumstances where mere mortals would not hesitate. Swinburne's answer is that although God knows more and is more able than me to ameliorate suffering, he refrains from acting despite the cries of the afflicted:

'Hence a God who sees far more clearly than we do the consequences of quarrels may have duties very different from ours with respect to such particular quarrels. He may know that the suffering that A will cause B is as nearly as great as these screams may suggest to us and will provide (unknown to us) an opportunity to C to help B recover and will thus give C a deep responsibility which he would not otherwise have' (*op. cit.*).

This is little short of offensive: readiness to be open-minded about such matters is a sign of a corrupt mind. There are screams and there are screams, and to ask what use are the screams of the innocent is to embark on a speculation we should not even contemplate. If there is a 'higher' form of reasoning among God and his angels, where such suffering is open for compromise and calculation, then so much the worse for God and his angels.

The theodicist's world is not the world in which I live. In my world, there are disasters of natural and moral kinds which strike without rhyme or reason. Where, if much can be done to influence character, much over which we have no control can also have such an influence.

The construction of a theodicy is the result of a confused view of what the relationship between the will of God and the lives of men and women must be.

A theodicy attempts to give reasons where reasons are inappropriate. One has to be ready in the face of one's cry: 'Why is this happening to me?' to reply: 'Why shouldn't it?' It is possible to trust in God and still see the pointlessness in suffering, as did Job, or as David did as he walked through the valley of the shadow of death; he could still trust God.

Theodicies are part of the rationalism which clouds our understanding of religious belief.

Talk of reasonableness and rationality is not the most natural response of most believers to the central tenets of their faith (as I have argued elsewhere: see *The Anatomy of Belief and Unbelief*, 2023). There is an urge, in some, to draw from the proposition that God is omnipotent that, as the word suggests, he can do anything. And this *doing* is often construed mechanistically. In another chapter, I show the difficulties of making sense of this anthropomorphism. The problem of evil is a contrivance we should avoid because it distorts the real nature of religious belief.

We are back with the notion that there is a divine agent who performs these actions. The only actions they embody are those that compose the natural events we are calling his acts. But what does it add to the description of these events to say that God does them?

The concept of divine agency requires us to postulate a divine mental life to give content to the belief that God acts.

If God is incorporeal, how can his worshippers identify him to refer to or, in particular, to address, if one assumes an unwillingness to identify him with the ancillary objects, such as altars, that are present when some acts of worship are performed?

Clearly no incorporeal being can be so distinguished, not just because he cannot be seen or *picked out* (individuated), but because in the absence of any *body* we cannot give content to the individuation of one such being from another, just as we cannot give content to the notion of some mental act being performed by the same incorporeal being who performed a previous one, rather than by another. But perhaps this only shows that it is incoherent (as indeed it is) to hold there could be a *plurality* of incorporeal (and particularly *omnipotent*) beings.

But what does all of this say of *karma*? It is sometimes suggested, as we have seen with Weber, that, say, Hinduism does not need to answer the problem of evil: the mechanism of *karma*, indeed, *karma's* mechanistic doctrine, explains the existence of evil in the world without needing to lay blame at the feet of the Gods: man, through *karma*, is the maker of his own suffering. There are, as we have seen, overwhelming flaws in this mechanistic view. Moreover, as I have shown above, the whole idea of a theodicy is confused anyway.

I shall now show that, logical ruminations aside, the doctrine of *karma* is morally flawed.

CHAPTER 7
Karma and ethics

John Gray says:

'Western thought is fixated on the gap between what *is* and what *ought to be*. In everyday life we do not scan our options beforehand, then enact the one that is best. We simply deal with whatever is at hand. We get up in the morning and put on our clothes without meaning to do so. We help a friend in just the same way. Different people follow different customs; but in acting without intention, we are not simply following habit. Intentional acts occur in all sorts of situations, including those we have never come across before' (*Straw Dogs,* 2002).

We must find some way of considering – or, indeed, of empowering – the place of moral considerations in our lives. Unless we do this, our assessment of human behaviour will be a caricature which would consist, in a fashion not unlike John Gray's, of a view of our behaviour as an administrative outlook on life. If someone believes, as Gray appears to do, that our moral behaviour is essentially our ability sensibly to control those areas of our lives where we can affect change – getting up in the morning and putting our clothes on – then our ethical outlook will be essentially administrative. How best to organize the socks draw. But this misses the point.

The question of the ways in which moral considerations place limits on human action is one which can never be far away from the central issues in moral philosophy. It is generally agreed that some account must be given of the limiting role of moral considerations. Since, without one, one is left with a mere caricature of human action. That caricature would consist, roughly, of a picture of human action as the calculation of the most efficient means of attaining predetermined ends. Within this context, of course, there is legitimate talk of limits. If, for example, a man has a purpose in mind, the very character of that purpose rules certain means out of consideration. It does so, not only by showing that some means are more effective than others in securing the desired end, but also in circumscribing a certain area of relevance so that courses of action which fall outside it will not even arise for consideration. Thus, if what I want to do is to avoid burglary, then various suggestions may be made to me about how I could achieve that end. I might be told to bolt the doors and windows; I might be encouraged to install an alarm; or I might be told to move to the South Pole. People would differ over the effectiveness of the means proposed, but not anything could count as possible advice. If someone told me to wear a certain coloured tie or go for a long walk, I might take this as a way of telling me to forget the purpose I had in mind, but I could not take it as a possible means of attaining that end. If it is likely that the law would impose a certain limit on the means one pursues to achieve a certain goal then it would be foolhardy to employ those means. But morality lies beyond this.

There is such a thing as moral praise and blame. There is a concern, not simply with working out the best ways of getting what we want, but with the character of our wants and the nature of our strivings to satisfy them. Here we have a limit placed on human action which is different in kind from the limits which our purposes play on the means we employ. The limits set by moral considerations constitute an additional principle of discrimination, since more is taken into account than our purposes and the best ways of achieving them. When purpose and its execution have had their say, there remains the question of whether such a course of action can be taken in the name of decency.

Moral considerations impose a limit on our purposes and their execution which the distinction between means and ends cannot account for, since means and ends alike come under moral scrutiny. This is not just a negative matter. If moral considerations condemn meanness, they also extol generosity; if they condemn drug-taking, they also commend a healthy lifestyle. Generosity, truthfulness, kindness, loyalty and not mere negations or restrictions, but positive virtues and ideals in human life which make for many that life worth living.

The discovery of what is morally possible for one in any situation is not the elevation of the good in an order of priority such that once the order is established one does not have to worry about the lower reaches of the scale. On the contrary, even after a person has decided what he must do in these situations, he may feel remorse for having committed the evil which his decision inevitably involved. When one lies to save a friend further suffering, despite the fact that one's whole relationship with him has been characterized by absolute straightforwardness and honesty; when one has to go against the wishes of parents who have sacrificed a great deal for one in deciding to marry a certain girl or to take up a certain job; when a man is forced to kill another person in order to save a child's life. Talk about establishing an order of goods would be a vulgar falsification for many people. They did what they had to do, but they did not glory in it. It is essential to recognize that in moral dilemmas, the discovery of what must be done often involves one in evil, pain and suffering.

The quality of our attachments is the quality of our understanding. Being dutiful involves being just; justice must make a pact with mercy. Plato's moral Forms cohere and interweave, making a *koinonia*, a fellowship. One point of certainty supports another. These mutual coherences of the values we feel sure of, and the things we desire, develop the thickening destiny of our lives. Here we may understand the feelings of Schopenhauer and Wittgenstein when they rejected 'duty' as a mere arbitrary listing of divinely commanded particular tasks, as opposed to a more general moral sensibility. Moral considerations have a superordinate bearing on purposes and their execution. If that is so, ethics stands resplendent beyond talk of means and purposes, or worse, custom and intentionless acts. Good and evil are *sui generis*.

For many believers, *karma* is mechanistic which, as we have seen above, may result in a thoroughgoing determinism. That being so, all the considerations above are obviated as morality is subsumed within the causal nexus of *karma* thus diminishing an appreciation of the depth of our lives and entailing an unfairness we should reject as immoral.

Consider a part of one of the Ten Commandments:

Exodus 20:5:

'... I, the Lord your God, am a jealous God, visiting the iniquity of the fathers upon the children to the third and fourth generation...'

I take it as axiomatic that punishing the innocent for crimes committed by others is evil. And, to paraphrase Elizabeth Anscombe, a willingness to consider judicially to punish the innocent shows a corrupt mind.

Tony Blair, then Prime Minister of the United Kingdom, on 15 March 2007, in a joint press conference with the Ghanaian President John Kufuor, apologized for Britain's role in the so-called Transatlantic 'slave trade': 'I have said we are sorry and I say it again... (It is important) to remember what happened in the past, to condemn it and say why it is entirely unacceptable.'

I take it as axiomatic that guilt is not inherited. The concept of collective 'white guilt' is currently quite fashionable: universities (which should know better), businesses, and celebrities fall over themselves to parade their racial blameworthiness. It is interesting that the black ancestors of black slave-runners (historically far more involved in and responsible for the slave trade than their white counterparts) are not clamouring to proclaim their guilt.

Herein lie two themes: first, emotional fraudulence. Clarion declarations, such as Tony Blair's, of moral dereliction do not have the texture of guilt; they draw attention to the *faux* guilt of the confessor; they are prideful. Elaborate racial apologies are a form of showing off.

As Lionel Shriver notes (*Spectator*, 11 July, 2020):

'We're witnessing the spectacle of white people frantically competing with other white people over who can appear more self-excoriating, more self-loathing. But these people don't hate themselves. They hate other people – mythical other people for the most part, all those terrible racist white folks to whom they can feel vastly superior…'

These confessions are defensive; they are diversionary and an attempt to opt out. Guilt, even worse, shame, feels bad. Shame can be soul-destroying. You don't parade your shame in public; you whisper it in the confessional.

Secondly, we are in danger of installing heritable guilt as morally valid. Now that we are to embrace the concept of an ineradicable 'systemic racism' (even in the Church of England, of all places), while employees take mandatory courses on 'unconscious bias', bigotry is no longer a sin we choose or refuse to perpetuate, but a stain handed down through generations: '… upon the children of the third and fourth generations…' Is this really what we want? Will we stick modern Mongolians with the rampages of twelfth century Genghis Khan? Do we hold some 19-year-old Muscovite today responsible for Stalin's gulags? Do we hold some 19-year-old Berliners responsible for the depredations of Adolf Hitler?

But maybe we should not be so selective. Forget talk about 'white people' (Russians, Jews, Scots, Armenians and Appalachian rednecks, Chatham chavs and Australian boguns) as if they are all equally culpable and equally relevant. Why not just talk about 'people'? As a species, we've been treating each other, other species, and the planet, in ways which can hardly be regarded as commendable. The horrors to which we've subjected each other, including slavery, but a great deal else, are so incomprehensibly awful that no one, as an individual, could conceivably bear the crushing weight of all that torture, mass murder and slaughter. If guilt is inherited, then every last one of us should be condemned to Dante's ninth circle of hell.

Contrary to the doctrine of *karma*, any advantages conferred at birth are not of our making. We had no part in determining the history which soaks the ground at our feet, let alone our own history.

It is irrational to feel guilt or shame about something we didn't do. It is immoral to lay guilt at the feet of those who are innocent of purported crimes. It is sensible to feel sorrow and abhorrence about the likes of slavery. But claiming that what happened before you were born is all your fault is not only ridiculous, it is vain.

We should feel nothing but utter moral disapprobation for those who are willing knowingly to punish the sins of others on innocent third parties. Likewise, we should feel nothing other than utter moral disapprobation for those attempting vaingloriously to appropriate blame for matters of which they are innocent.

What are we then to say of moral approbation in respect of the doctrine of *karma* where it appears that someone other than the guilty party is punished for their sins? If, for example, Smith^b at T^2 suffers a 'lower' rebirth because of the actions of Smith^a at T^1? The answer, it will be said, is clear in that it is Smith, a continuing entity, who is punished for *his* sins, not someone else's. For this to be the case, we should have to be able to identify Smith^a *as the same person* as Smith^b, and that, as we have seen in our consideration of disembodied existence above, we cannot do.

Another line of defence might be that Smith^b being punished for

Smith[a]'s sins is somehow mitigated by the fact that Smith[a] knows he will at some, indefinite time in the future be punished for his offences. I have examined the logic of karmic causality in respect of such possible foreknowledge and found it to be incoherent.

We must conclude, therefore, that the logic of karmic causality, its possible individuation in specific cases, and its moral turpitude, mean that it, as a doctrine, is fundamentally flawed; it is deserving of our moral disapprobation.

CHAPTER 8

Karma and Vegetarianism

I saw a poster advertising a concert featuring the Smyths, entitled *Meat is Murder*. Talk of rights, whether of humans or of other animals, is neither here nor there. If meat were murder, if we ate our own dead, then there might be some point in the analogy, but we don't.

So why don't we eat our dead? And why are we unwilling to kill our fellows for food? And are the reasons we don't eat our dead or kill our fellows for food relevant to arguments about not eating animals? Evolutionary theory and the seemingly ubiquitous stream of wildlife programmes have distorted our view of the natural world: we are *not* as other animals. For the most part, we do not kill younger members of our social groupings if they are sired by rival males, as gorillas sometimes do; nor do we hunt down members of species close to our own in the way chimpanzees do to Colobus monkeys. We should question seriously our phoney (or at least hypocritical) sentimentality towards other animals. On the other hand, we should be in no doubt whatsoever about the rapacious nature of humans both in respect of the environment, including other animals, and of each other. But that is not the point: we can be certain that meat is not murder.

Other animals can't be ascribed the mental states that can be ascribed to humans. Other animals can't, for example, feel remorse: to do that we have to be able to feel that we have failed to do what we should have done and this also turns on other notions: obligation, concern for others, and so on. And all this is only possible because of thought capable of generating infinite possibilities of meaning and fact in a way that is extraordinarily efficient.

Not long ago – in evolutionary terms – our ancestors were monkeys. 125,000 years ago, in the Eemian interglacial period, the earth was warmer than it is now and humans as we now know them didn't exist. *Homo sapiens*, in an earlier incarnation of at least three hominids, appeared in Africa about 200,000 years ago. But at about 100,000 years ago, humans as we now know them broke the chain of dependence of natural evolution and started the irreversible dichotomy between humans and other animals. Were it not for humans, we would now have a different biosphere – forests, savannas, glaciers, with an earth teeming with large land animals and heaving seas.

125,000 years ago, had there been no humans there would now be another ice age. Although there is the other theory – convergent evolution – that if we humans hadn't brought about this devastation then other species thrown up by evolution would have done so; the *what if* theory.

Once humans opposed the nature of which they were a part and colonized the world, beginning in the Ancient Near East 100,000 years ago, South Asia 50,000 years ago, Europe 43,000 years ago, my native Australia 40,000 years ago, and the Americas between 30 and 15,000 years ago, the devastation that followed was inevitable. Had they not done so, there would not be the unprecedented extinctions that we have seen since then.

I am nothing but my cells. I am composed of nothing but my cells and I am host to millions of bacteria. The cells which collectively compose me are not aware of me, in much the same way that a gnat does not know it is a gnat. My awareness of myself is a difference *in kind* from me and other animals.

It is language that has enabled us to break the prison of our instincts. As Christopher Booker says:

'We have become free to imagine how all these (instinctual urges) can be done differently. Whereas one ant colony is structured like any other, the forms of human organization may vary as widely as a North Korean dictatorship and a village cricket club.

'It is our ability to escape from the rigid frame of instinct which explains almost everything that distinguishes human beings from any other form of life.'

Some vegetarians try to justify their unwillingness to eat meat on the ground that eating meat is morally equivalent to eating humans – that animals share the basic rights we do. They seem not to see any anomaly in not eating animals that have died of natural causes or accidentally, but let that pass.

But if they concede that eating people is not something one does, then talk of the rights of animals becomes another, different issue.

Rai Gaita says:

'Like the impossibility that we should consign our dead to the rubbish collection or that we should routinely number rather than name our children, they are impossibilities that structure and are structured by that part of the realm of meaning in which reality is embedded... It is in the imaginative appreciation of surface similarities between the bodies of pregnant women and animals, and in the surface similarities of their behaviour, rather than in the investigation of biological causes of maternal behaviour, that we discover the creaturely nature we have in common. When we look more closely at our behaviour and the behaviour of animals, however, we also see important differences that are revealed in the fact that our behaviour, but not that of animals, is often determined by reflection on its meaning.

'... The concept of unconditional love has no application to animals no matter how devotedly they care for their young or how ferociously they protect them at risk to their own lives.

We can love unconditionally only because we can impose – consciously or unconsciously – conditions on our love and be answerable for the fact that we do it' (*A Common Humanity*, 2000).

Humans and animals are different, not just in terms of what, or who, we are willing to eat. That animals communicate does not even begin to show that they speak; they do not share a concern for truth or honesty of speech and the demands that such things make upon our lives, and until they do such things they are not even engaged in the kind of thing that humans do when they 'communicate'.

Are dogs baptized? Are humans culled? Why is sodomy a taboo? Why is it permissible to eat other animals and yet not to have sex with them? One must examine the reason why humans and animals are treated differently. And this has to be seen against a background where people reverse the normal moral agenda: where the interests of 'nature', including other animals, are promoted over those of humans, e.g., where action – or lack of it – taken in the name of, say, biodiversity, entails that flood plains are subject to increasing flooding. In other words, reverse discrimination in favour of other animals.

Cora Diamond shows that it is not out of respect for the interests of animals that we treat, say, pets as we do:

'Treating pets in these ways is not at all a matter of recognizing some interest which pets have in being so treated. There is not a class of beings, pets, whose nature, whose capacities, are such that we owe it to them to treat them in these ways... It is not out of respect for our interests which is involved in our not eating each other... We learn what a human being is in – among other ways – sitting at a table where we eat them. We are around the table and they are on it' ('Eating Meat and Eating People', *The Realistic Spirit*, 2001).

Diamond notes that we formed the idea of the difference between animals and people knowing 'perfectly well the overwhelming obvious similarities'. But a starting point for understanding the difference has to be understanding why we don't eat people.

We have never truly embraced the Copernican revolution: we are still the centre of the universe in all respects. Gray says that we are only one animal among many; he is wrong: we are different *in kind*.

And, of course, our view of each of these responses will vary from person-to-person and society-to-society.

How we treat animals, according to conceptions of rightness or justice, will be finely nuanced in a way that Gray is not: 'Where humans differ from ravens is that they use language to look back on their lives and call up a virtual self' (*Straw Dogs*, 2002).

Again, Diamond says:

'I should say that the notion of a fellow creature is extremely labile, and that is partly because it is not something over and above the extension of such concepts as justice, charity and friendship-or-companionship-or-cordiality.'

Behind part of this is the metaphysical difficulty of getting behind an animal's behaviour to its mind, whether it is a non-human animal or a human one. It is in these conceptions that our relations with animals consist, whereas Gray puts this on its head: 'The roots of ethics are in animal virtues'.

Think, for example, of the idea of an animal as a pest. In Australia, kangaroos are widely recognized as pests – especially by the farming community where they are mainly to be found – and shot. We hear of grey (but interestingly not red) squirrels as rats with bushy tails, or of pigeons as sky rats or rats with wings. To call an animal 'a pest' is to isolate it from other animals, excluding it from considerations of treatment involving rights etc. In Manhattan and Central London and Wimbledon, hawks are now 'employed' to kill pigeons. Rats and other vermin are poisoned. But when someone poisons a dog or a cat, prosecution ensues. Dogs and cats are not pests. But rats are animals.

It is worth here quoting Gaita at length. This passage comes from a chapter, *An attitude towards a soul*, where he is discussing 'our sense of the *reality* of another human being' and, in particular, the ways in which we might feel pity for our fellow creatures:

'When we pity a creature in pain we do not pity an 'entity' in pain of such and such severity. Our pity takes a more substantial object. When it is for a human being it is irreducibly for a human being. I do not mean merely that if we pity a human being, then it is that human being we pity, and if we pity a dog then it is that dog. I mean that when we pity a human being in pain then we pity him, irreducibly, as a human being, whereas if we pity a dog, then we pity it not as a dog but as an animal of a certain kind, which would include cats and horses, though not worms. When we pity a human being, our pity for him is different from our pity for a dog, because a human being suffers other things in addition to his pain. It is different because of *the meaning* pain can have on human life and because of what a human life can mean. An animal in severe pain is 'put out of its misery'. Even when, as was reported of an Argentinian soldier who fell into a fire in the Falklands, a human being is killed so that he will be spared further suffering, he is not killed in the same spirit as we would shoot a horse. It is not that we feel differently about it, that we find it more difficult, or that we feel more sorrow. That is not what is most significant. What is most significant is the descriptions, the categories of meaning, under which we understand our reluctance and our sorrow and what we are doing. The Argentinian soldier was not eaten afterwards. That fact, and many others of the same kind, determine what the shooting was' (*Good and Evil: An Absolute Conception*, 2004).

Gaita quotes the oft-repeated story, from Orwell's *Looking Back on the Spanish War*, when he found himself unable to shoot the enemy soldier who ran by holding up his trousers:

'I had come here to shoot at 'Fascists'; the man who is holding up his trousers isn't a 'fascist', he is visibly a fellow creature, similar to yourself, and you don't feel like shooting at him.'

Gaita calls Orwell's response 'a spontaneous expression of a sense of common humanity'. Just as there is a complex matrix of responses to animals so also there is to our fellow human beings as the tensions between enemy (fascist) and fellow creature (man holding up his trousers) in Orwell's story demonstrates.

One should note here, however, that Orwell's reaction to the man holding up his trousers is a psychological one. It is important to differentiate between psychological and moral responses. For example, there is what might be called the 'thin-end-of-the-wedge' argument: if, for example, you agree to some form of eugenics, you are you well on your way to some kind of Holocaust. While this has a certain psychological force, there is no logic to it. Ethics is, after all, in part, about drawing lines and it is relatively easy to draw a line between some kind of eugenical machinations and those of the Holocaust. Here the 'thin-end-of-the-wedge' argument has a psychological force but really says nothing particularly insightful about the morality of such matters. As Gaita says:

'The sharp distinction between the moral and psychological, and the tendency to think that expressions of moral impossibility are really misleading ways of expressing a sense of obligation, are aspects of what could be called meaning-neglect. But the interdependencies between modalities of possibility and necessity, and coming to see the meaning of something, go beyond what is called morality' (*op. cit.*).

Meaning, of which morality is a part, arises from *human* interaction, the culture of being human. We can be certain that eating a human being is worse than eating an animal, but it is also *different in kind*.

I do not claim this simply because of the difference in the visceral reaction we might expect to someone who served up babies for dinner as opposed to, say, veal. Nor do I mean that the rights of animals are of less consequence than the rights of man. There is no such thing as rights. To have a right to something implies that it would be morally wrong to deprive anyone of it without sufficient justification. Whilst such 'rights' (e.g. life, liberty, and the pursuit of happiness) are sometimes referred to as *natural* rights, in fact, no rights exist in nature.

To say that some action is unjust because someone's rights have been violated does nothing to explain why it is unjust, nor does it strengthen the charge that it is unjust by resorting to talk of rights. Indeed, such talk is often ludicrously inadequate. We all do well to listen to these wise words of Simone Weil, a woman who lived and died fighting oppression:

'If you say to someone who has ears to hear: "What you are doing to me is not just", you may touch and awaken at its source the spirit of attention and love. But it is not the same with words like "I have the right to..." Or "You have the right to..." They evoke a latent war and awaken the spirit of contention. To place the notion of rights at the centre of social conflict is to inhibit any possible impulse of charity on both sides.

'Relying almost exclusively on this notion, it becomes impossible to keep one's eyes on the real problem. If someone tries to browbeat a farmer to sell his eggs at a moderate price, the farmer can say: "I have the right to keep my eggs if I don't get a good enough price." But if a young girl is being forced into a brothel she will not talk about her rights. In such a situation the word would sound ludicrously inadequate' ('Human Personality', *The Simone Weil Reader*, 1977).

The difference in kind can be seen if we return to my earlier discussion of killing animals which are pests. There are simply no circumstances in which *any* human being whose crimes are so heinous and whose character is so evil that he can be killed as one would kill a pest; this I take to be a *moral absolute* embedded in the realm of *meaning* which is a form of *human* interaction.

Gaita:

'The reasons why the allies fought against Germany are complex, but many people believe rightly that the Holocaust itself would have proved sufficient reason. But... no-one responds, and I think no-one can seriously wish to respond, to the slaughter of animals as though it justified taking up arms against farmers, butchers and people who work in abattoirs. That can hardly be irrelevant to how we should understand the moral character of our indifference to the slaughter of animals. It must also inform the moral character of any other analogies we may be tempted to draw between the Holocaust and our treatment of animals. People have said that the Holocaust and the way we now kill animals are examples of the 'industrialization of death', as though the radical differences between Auschwitz and a modern abattoir do not deprive the comparison of power to shed light' (*op. cit.*).

Another way of looking at man's relation with other animals is to turn to the Eastern tradition and, in particular, the doctrine of *ahimsa*, founded in the Hindu notion that all life is a unity: it means renunciation of the will to kill or damage.

The idea of *ahimsa* (harmlessness, non-injury or non-violence) is best exemplified in the thought of Mahatma Gandhi who characterized it by its more positive aspects: friendliness and compassion.

The first occurrence of the word in Sanskrit literature is in the C.U. (3.17.4) where it is given as an instance of one of the five ethical virtues (austerity, almsgiving, uprightness, *harmlessness*, truthfulness). The doctrine reaches its apotheosis with respect to the cow, an animal which in some parts of Hinduism has a special sanctity, entitling it not only to protection but also to worship. The much later *Laws of Manu* – bizarrely – seem not only to endorse *ahimsa* but also man-eating: it is permissible to eat consecrated flesh.

Ahimsa is generally thought to have originated with the Jains and the Buddhists, being later adopted by Brahmanic Hinduism after it began to win its way in North India where Buddhism was developed. Of course, in Jainism, the slaying of any creature is forbidden. It may well be that the doctrine was also influenced by a magico-ritualistic dread of destroying life in any form.

It seems that, along with the doctrine of *ahimsa*, so also grew the doctrine of the soul or self (*atman*) as well as that of *karma*. It is quite possible that the idea of *ahimsa* sprang from the conception that the same self which dwells in oneself also dwelt in other beings and that by injuring other beings one would injure oneself (or one's fellow). This notion, when combined with the doctrine of *samsara*, the transmigration of souls, can easily lead to the conclusion that the eater of meat is the eater of souls: *meat is murder*. Indeed, in some of the legal texts of *Manu*, we encounter the idea that the eater of meat of an animal will be eaten by that animal in the next world. Either way, the notion of the soul and rebirth played an important part in the formulation of the doctrine of *ahimsa*.

The issue reaches a critical point in the *Bhagavadgita* where Lord Krishna, disguised as a charioteer, tells Arjuna, a prince, that it is his duty to prosecute a just war and to kill the enemy, his cousins. To convince the reluctant Arjuna, Lord Krishna argues that the embodied self is immortal and is not destroyed when the body is destroyed and that what is born must die and what dies must be born again; this is coupled with the fact that it is the duty (*dharma*) of the princely (*kshatriya*) class to fight a just war. It is easy to extrapolate from here to the doctrines of *atman*, *samsara* and *ahimsa*. Arjuna must pursue the battle; it is his duty.

In the *Yagnavalkya* sections of the *Brhadaranyaka Upanishad*, we find the idea of renunciation being the result of the knowledge that good deeds done in this world bear fruit in the next world and in future births; this fate can be overcome only by realizing the unity of all beings in the universal self. Avoiding harm to all living beings is the best means to obtain union with the universal self. The universal self can be best seen in the *Gita* where the self is thought of as a timeless *monad*, and also a minute part of Brahman.

As will be evident, this teaching involves ethical norms of a radically different type to that of the West. The ethical dictum: *Thou shalt not kill*, and its corollaries regarding non-injury or harm to others (and self) is of singular importance in Western culture, which sees such principles as being universally valid since the time of the mythological institution of the Decalogue on Sinai by Moses. It is common to regard *ahimsa* as an ethical equivalent to the commandments of Moses and to assume a Hindu will accord it equal value. Such bombast misconstrues the gravamen of the *Gita*.

While the doctrine of *ahimsa* may be seen as a guide to the ethical conundrum of eating animals, it is so overladen with the wrong-headed, metaphysical superstructure of *karma* and *samsara* as to be unhelpful as a basis for any ethical ruminations.

On the other hand, Gandhi's take on *ahimsa* as compassion is to be commended, although *that* is obvious.

In 2004, 'animal liberation' activists bullied and terrorized a construction firm into pulling out of a contract to build a new medical research lab for Oxford University. Similar tactics were used in the same year to close down Cambridge University's proposed primate research lab.

Under British law, animal experimentation is only allowed for the purposes of serious medical research and where there is no realistic alternative. As far as the extremists are concerned, animals have just as many rights as humans (including the right to become members of a trades union?). And liberating them from the vivisectionist is therefore a moral imperative. And yet animals have no moral sense. Either way, such moral turpitude, including criminal acts and death threats, beggars belief.

Britain is seen as a pioneer in the field of animal rights as it once was in the field of animal welfare. The Karl Marx of the animal-rights movement is the Australian, Harvard-based, utilitarian philosopher, Peter Singer, whose book *Animal Liberation* (1976) is seen by many as the movement's Bible: he promotes 'equal consideration of interests' between humans and other animals.

Some think that the rise of this kind of thinking follows the collapse of traditional religion where belief in the immortal soul conferred an automatic moral ascendancy over the rest of nature; others see it as the authority conferred on man by God as steward of the world and its resources, including other animals.

The notion of a human being as having a soul (while other animals do not) is a confused one. As with so much metaphysical speculation, talk of the soul as an entity, whether of humans or other animals, is misguided. But there are other ways of speaking about souls, particularly in our poets, that are neither metaphysical speculation nor trivial: 'As the hart longs for flowing streams, so longs my soul for thee, O God' (*Psalm* 42). It is not insignificant that the hart may long for flowing streams but it would be ridiculous to suggest that it longs for God. The soul's longing for God is part of the spiritual life that men may enjoy but which is not part of the life of other animals. But to speak in this way is not to suggest the existence of a metaphysical entity: only human beings have a capacity for spirituality and that is because we are able to reflect on what it is to be human and to rejoice in the many responses that that contemplation evinces. Such responses are not possible for other animals. It is only when we are capable of such responses, amongst other things, that we can be said to have a soul; it speaks, in part, of what it is to be human.

The motivation for vegetarianism that arises from *karma* is based on a confusion.

CHAPTER 9

Karma in Popular Literature

I shall look at two modern books on karma: one, firmly in the Hindu tradition; the other arising from Tibetan Buddhism. In the first (*Karma – A Yogi's Guide to Crafting Your Destiny*, Sadhguru, Penguin, 2021), we have the whole notion of *karma* framed differently. It is not: '… to do with reward and punishment. It has nothing to do with some despotic life author up in the sky, working with the primitive devices of carrot and stick…' (p. 7f). It is, rather: '… we are the makers of our own fate… Karma is about becoming the source of one's own creation' (p. 8). More particularly: 'Karma is not a creed, a scripture, and ideology, a philosophy or a theory. It is simply the way things are' (p. 8).

Karma, we are told, does not refer to *physical* deeds. Rather, it is about action in *body*, *mind* and *energy*. And that whatever you do on these three levels leaves a residue or imprint on you. *Karma* is a mechanism, functioning in much the same way that other bodily mechanisms do: we are offered the analogy of software.

Karma, too, operates in cycles: 'As the length of a karmic cycle decreases, life becomes progressively more unbalanced.' We should be aiming for the 'solar cycle', a period of 4,356 days.

The *karma* mechanism continues irrespective of circumstances, even death, and without yogic intervention, the grip of *karma* becomes bondage: 'This is the deadly tedium and tyranny of the karmic rut.'

In short, the karmic mechanism 'leaves a certain imprint' on your body, mind and energy: 'These imprints configure themselves into tendencies. These tendencies have been traditionally described in India by a wonderfully apt word: *vasana*. Literally, *vasana* means "smell". This "smell" is generated by a vast accumulation of impressions caused by your physical, mental, emotional and energy actions. Depending upon the type of "smell" you emit, you attract certain kinds of life situations to yourself' (p. 17). Your 'smell' depends on the kind of residual memory or karmic content to carry.

On the foundation of this deterministic model of *karma*, more extensive foundations are laid. Although never far from the Indian scriptures, Sadhguru attempts to interpret *karma* in the light of 21st-century living and demands. We are taken into further complexities of the model: *karma* and volition. In response to explaining the existence of evil/suffering: 'The cause of human suffering is oneself' (p. 37). Your *karma* is the way you respond to what is happening to you.

Time and again, we are told that *karma* is related only to cause and effect. Suffering and misery are always by choice. And '... the source of your misery is not your past actions...[it] is how you're processing the imprint of the past now' (p. 42).

Karma can be collective: the suffering within you comes not just from your individual past; it comes from your forefathers and will be transmitted to your unborn children.

What you call fate is just a life situation you have created for yourself unconsciously. What happened 2500 years ago is still imprinted in your body. But not only us, 'we carry the memories of our ancestors within us' (p. 62). '... Everything about it is the result of programming, from its shape and colour to its texture and size. This is why you still have your great-grandmother's arthritic knee and find it difficult to erase your monkey ancestor's habits! (Don't forget: a human being and a chimp share 98.6 percent of their DNA!)' (p. 68).

We hear of 'accumulated *karma*', of 'allotted *karma*', of 'actionable *karma* in the present' and 'actionable *karma* in the future' which latter perpetuates human cycles of compulsive action leading to cycles of birth and death. We are told how Karma Yoga can be a process of liberation. And thereafter the book describes practical ways this might be achieved.

All in all, *A Yogi's Guide*, is a modern, orthodox look at *karma* with a view to helping its readers navigate its, sometimes, labyrinthine paths.

Karma – What it Is; What it Isn't & Why it Matters, by Traleg Kyabgon (with a foreword by His holiness the Seventeenth Karmapa. The Karmapa is the head of the Karma Kagyu, the largest sub-section of one of the four major schools of Tibetan Buddhism. The historical seat of the Karmapas is the Tsurphu Monastery in the Tolung valley of Tibet) is firmly in the tradition of Tibetan Buddhism.

For Kyabgon, '... The Buddha defined karma as action, in the sense that we ourselves are responsible for our own condition in the world and that our thoughts and actions... determine our future. We are a product of causes and conditions – we are what we are due to past actions...' (p. 7). And 'Buddhism is distinctly different from other beliefs systems... by virtue of the fact that it has no divine being making or maintaining the order of the world' (p. 10).

Unlike its predecessor Hinduism, Buddhism teaches that '... we carry mixed karma and that we process our karma gradually and incrementally' (p. 26). Moreover, the apparent determinism of Hinduism's karma needs to be nuanced: 'Buddha did not regard karma as an inexorable law, almost mechanical in operation. Rather, he gave elasticity to the causal mechanism of its operation... An existing cause did not necessarily mean an effect would ensue, or that it would ensue in exact and direct proportion to the cause' (p. 34). While evident in Hinduism, Buddhism places great importance on the end-of-life: '... Of all mentation done in our life, of paramount significance is what we think about at the time of our death' (p. 35).

Buddhism does not, contrary to popular opinion, believe in reincarnation: 'Essentially, reincarnation refers to exactly the same person's coming back in another life, and this involves the idea of there being an intrinsic self, a soul. The Buddhist theory of rebirth does not posit that exactly the same person subsequently takes on a different life after death... As the Buddha himself explained, it is "the same but different". It is the notion of continuity that is addressed here, rather than a fixed kind of entity persisting and being transferred from one state of existence to another' (p. 43f).

But the notion of *moksha* or release into *nirvana* is still the goal: '... aiming not only to overcome negative karma but also positive karma. Both kinds of karma lead to rebirth, and it is the exhaustion of our karmic propensities that is the ultimate aim' (p. 73).

Kyabgon engages in what to many might appear obscure doctrinal and parochial disputation, e.g. the Yogacara (Cittamatra) school versus the Madhyamaka in the Mahayana tradition (p. 59ff). He is also given to the occasional, impenetrable verbiage: 'For Nagajuna, karma does not have true reality because it is devoid of inherent existence, yet karma does manifest. It is a manifest phenomenon; to that extent, it is real, it exists' (p. 79).

In spite of his nuancing equivocations over the nature of the person, i.e. no soul versus identity, we see in what follows that such apparently arbitrary differences can be, he claims, more than accounted for.

In their attempts to make *karma* accessible, both Sadhguru and Kyabgon employ modern analogies with frequent recourse to philosophical notions which are, at times, stretched so much that they mislead. Both are apologetical, i.e. they often argue their case against unseen and unknown opponents.

In spite of the attempted nuances and apparent modernity of both offerings, they still face the same challenges to which I have alluded in previous chapters.

CHAPTER 10
Karma and Death

In Hindu and Buddhist belief, death is seen in terms of the cycle of rebirths (*samsara*); this is endless unless release (*moksha*) from the cycle is attained. This release is to *nirvana*. Nirvana is not, contrary to popular opinion, heaven, or bliss, or paradise. Rather, *nirvana* is, in Buddhism, the extinguishing of the flame of the self while in Hinduism it is, according to the *Gita*, a state of peace shared eternally with Lord Krishna or, in some other scriptures or schools of thought, absorption into the all-being of *Brahman*: *sa va ayam atma brahma* (it, this atman, is most truly Brahman).

Brahman is outside the mundane world of birth and rebirth: it is the beginning and the end: '... atman is Brahman: already within us *is* the imperturbable, unchanging 'isness' of what there is, even when it is not' (Bowker, *The Meanings of Death*, 1991).

Viewed theistically, Brahman may be seen to be God, or viewed impersonally, as the absolute source of all that is. It is in this context that *karma* is the impersonal manifestation of consequence.

'That's how you are' is a translation of a Sanskrit phrase: '*Tat tvam asi*'. There is a truth which underlies all things and its essence is identical with one's own self (*atman*) and this self is the life force (*brahman*) within the world and humanity.

Apart from the question of the 'endless' cycle of rebirths, we have not considered the question of the nature of heaven, or indeed, of *nirvana*. There are reasons for believing that, at root, the notion of heaven is fundamentally unsatisfying or, at worst, incoherent. Julian Barnes explores this in his novel *A History of the World in 10½ Chapters* (2009).

A man awakes (having obviously died) to find that all his fondest wishes are not only anticipated but more than fulfilled. After a while, it becomes clear to him that he is in heaven. Gradually, and at first by accretion, his wishes become more extravagant and initially have to do with food, sex, golf, meeting famous people and shopping. In all these activities, 'you don't get tired – just kind of sated'. Eventually, all things he hopes for and imagines he wants are fulfilled (all his fantasies are mundane – he is not very imaginative) yet he feels an unease:

'I think it was the golf that made me [search] for some explanations. There was no doubt about it, over the months and years I played that lovely, lush course with its little tricks and temptations (how many times I put the ball in the water at the short eleventh!), my game improved no end. I said as much one day to Severiano, my regular caddy: "My game has improved no end." He agreed, and it was not until later, between dinner and sex, that I began to reflect on what I'd said. I had opened up on the course with a 67, and gradually my score was coming down. A while ago I was shooting a regular 59, and now, under cloudless skies, I was inching down to the low 50s... I could see my target score coming down through the 40s, then – a key psychological moment this – breaking the barrier of 36, that's to say two strokes a hole average, then coming down through the 20s. *My game has improved no end*, I thought, and repeated the words *no end* to myself. But that's, of course, exactly what it couldn't do: there had to be an end to my improvement. One day I would play a round of golf in 18 shots, I'd buy Severiano a couple of drinks, celebrate later with sturgeon and chips and sex – and then what? Had anyone, even here, ever played a golf course in 17 shots?'

His feeling of unease increases, even as he tries ever new and more extravagant experiences:

' - I went on several cruises;
- I learned canoeing, mountaineering, ballooning;
- I got into all sorts of danger and escaped;
- I explored the jungle;
- I watched a court case (didn't agree with the verdict);
- I tried being a painter (not as bad as I thought!) and a surgeon;
- I fell in love, of course, lots of times;
- I pretended I was the last person on earth (and the first).'

In spite of these adventures his unease grows until he discovers, not surprisingly, that others before him have felt the same sense of ennui and 'then they take up the option to die off'. He is shocked: 'So ... even religious people, who come here to worship God throughout eternity ... they end up throwing in the towel after a few years, hundred years, thousand years?' To which the answer is: 'Certainly'. He is even more surprised to learn that, eventually, everyone chooses this course: 'Over many thousands of years, calculated by old time, of course. But yes, everyone takes the option, sooner or later'. He concludes: 'After a while, getting what you want all the time is very close to not getting what you want all the time'.

J.S. Mill, more succinctly, offers the same warning:

'It is not only possible but probable that in a higher, and above all, happier condition of human life, not annihilation but immortality may be the burdensome idea; and that human nature, though pleased with the present, and by no means impatient to quit it, would find comfort and not sadness in the thought that it is not chained through eternity to a conscious existence which it cannot be assured that it will always wish to preserve' (*Three Essays*, 1887).

Maybe the Buddhist sense of annihilation in *nirvana* is the more to be desired?

But what sense can we make of life after death? There seems to be a belief abroad that belief in dualism (belief in the possibility of disembodied existence) is more compatible with belief in immortality than is materialism (with its only viable option, as we have seen, being contemporaneous resurrection). But as I have argued, dualism makes no sense. Where are we left? We may reject dualism on either of two grounds: the conceptual (as I have attempted to do above), or the empirical, where there are seen to be overwhelming grounds for believing it to be false.

As regards the former, we must consider the point, to which I alluded earlier, that even if disembodied existence were coherent, it would necessarily result in solipsism. It is worth here quoting Strawson at length:

'... from within our actual conceptual scheme, each of us can quite intelligibly conceive of his or her individual survival of bodily death. The effort of imagination is not even great. One has simply to think of oneself as having thoughts and memories as at present, visual and auditory experiences largely as at present, even, perhaps – though this involves certain complications – some quasi-tactual and organic sensations as at present, whilst (a) having no perceptions of a body related to one's experience as one's own body, and (b) having no power of initiating changes in the physical condition of the world, such as one does at present with one's hands, shoulders, feet and vocal chords. Condition (a) must be expanded by adding that no one else exhibits reactions indicating that he perceives a body at the point which one's body would be occupying if one were seeing and hearing in an embodied state from the point from which one is seeing and hearing in a disembodied state. One could, of course, imagine condition (a) being fulfilled, in both its parts, without condition (b) being fulfilled. This would be a rather vulgar fancy, in the class of the table-tapping spirits with familiar voices. But suppose we take disembodiment strictly in the sense that we imagine both (a) and (b) fulfilled. Then two consequences follow, one of which is commonly noted, the other of which is perhaps insufficiently attended to. The first is that the strictly disembodied individual is strictly solitary, and it must remain for him indeed an utterly empty, though not meaningless, speculation, as to whether there are any other members of his class. The other, and less commonly noticed point, is that in order to retain his idea of himself as an individual, he must always think of himself as *dis*embodied, as a *former* person. That is to say, he must contrive still to have the idea of himself as a member of a class or type of entities with whom, however, he is now debarred from entering into any of those transactions the past fact of which was the condition of his having any idea of himself at all. Since then he has, as it were, no personal life of his own to lead, he must live much in the memories of the personal life he did lead; or he might, when this living in the past loses its appeal, achieve some kind of attenuated vicarious personal experience by taking a certain kind of interest in the human affairs of which he is a mute and invisible witness… At the limit of attenuation there is, *from the point of view of his survival as an individual*, no difference between the continuance of experience and its cessation. Disembodied survival, on such terms as these, may well seem unattractive. No doubt it is for this reason that the orthodox have wisely insisted on the resurrection of the body' (*Individuals*, op. cit.).

De facto solipsism aside, and following the tradition that immaterial substances (disembodied persons) lack spatial properties, we might contend that this considerable lack renders that notion of immaterial substances incoherent. How else could such substances be individuated? Nor could the notion of identity through time apply to properties lacking spatio-temporality. We would need to be able to imagine that there could non-spatial relationships between immaterial substances (say, minds) and material substances (say, bodies) which play a role in determining what causal relationships can hold between these substances which is an analogy as to the role which spatial relationships play in determining what causal relationships can hold between material substances. And this, I contend, cannot be imagined.

I have argued elsewhere (*The Anatomy of Belief and Unbelief, op. cit.*) that if one can show that the possibility of having some kind of inner life depends on there being common activities in a common language, then any attempt to identify the essence of the self – mind, soul, spirit, call it what you will – with an inner substance divorced from such connections, can be shown to be radically confused.

D.Z. Phillips says:

'Talk about the soul... is not talk about some strange sort of "thing". On the contrary, it is a kind of talk bound up with certain moral or religious reflections a man may make on the life he is leading. Once this is recognized, once one ceases to think of the soul as a thing, as some kind of incorporeal substance, one can be brought to see that in certain contexts talk about the soul is a way of talking about human beings' (*Death and Immortality*, 1970).

Talk of a cycle of rebirths, or of the immortality of the soul, can thus be seen to be other than disquisitions on whether one survives one's death; it can be seen to be an attempt to place eternal life in a moral or religious context. Thus, eternity ceases to be life of infinite duration but, as with Plato's absolutes, a means by which this life is judged, is seen as *sub species aeternitatis*. As Wittgenstein says: 'Not only is there no guarantee of the temporal immortality of the human soul, that is to say of its eternal survival after death; but, in any case, this assumption completely fails to accomplish the purpose for which it has always been intended. Or is some riddle solved by my surviving forever? Is not this eternal life itself as much of a riddle as our present life? The solution of the riddle of life in space and time lies *outside* space and time' (6.4312 *Tractatus Logico-Philosophicus*).

If I say I survive my death, I do not know what I am saying. Who, after all, is this 'I'? MacKinnon says:

'Do I suppose that "I" is the name of a kind of ultimate substrate of qualities, clad with its states much as a clothes-horse is draped with towels, shirts, etc.? Do I think that I am related to my biography in that kind of way? Yet much of our superficial talk about survival suggest that we do. Whether we think of survival, or of the survivor, we are at once plunged into bewilderment' (*New Essays in Philosophical Theology*, 1955).

The answer to this question must be: of course! We *are* plunged into bewilderment. How can such objects as people survive physical dissolution?

Geach sheds light on the 'I': 'In communication with others, a man uses "I" in expressing his mental states in order that others may learn who is in pain or puzzled or what not; it is natural that he should still use "I" in soliloquy when expressing these states, but his "I" has not now the role of telling *himself* who is in pain or puzzled. It no longer refers to a person or a human being; just as "there" in "There is a difference between pride and vanity" has no longer the role of referring to a place; or again, the *"es"* in the German idiom *"es gibt"* (corresponding to "there is": literally "it gives") no longer refers to a giver' (*op. cit.*).

Geach's conclusion is that 'memory could in no case give content to an idea of reincarnation'.

Again, Wittgenstein: 'Our life is endless as the visual field is without limit. Death is not an event in life. Death is not lived through.' Outside the visual field nothing is seen, not even darkness: for whatever is seen is seen within the visual field. When we are dead, nothing is experienced, not even emptiness: for there is no one to experience. For each of us 'the world in death does not change, but ceases' (*Tractatus*, 6.431 and 6.1411).

AFTERWORD

In this book, I have argued, among other things, that *karma* entails belief in either disembodied persons or a series of contemporaneously resurrected persons; both these notions are radically confused and, in the main, incoherent. I have also argued that the doctrine is, as it is often presented, morally repugnant and unhelpful when thinking about death.

In an earlier work, *The Anatomy of Belief and Unbelief*, I argued that propositional belief has scant place in religion. Unfortunately, this cannot be said of the doctrine of *karma* which occupies a central place in the thinking of Hindus and Buddhists, among others.

In the popular conception of *karma*, the doctrine amounts to little more than the idea that 'you reap what you sow'. But this notion is obvious: actions have consequences.

As I said in *The Anatomy of Belief and Unbelief*: 'Causes rarely provide meanings ... But religion is a strange sediment in human consciousness - which itself might have an evolutionary cause - and trying to understand it is a worthy cause ...there are plenty of religions in which belief in the gods is a hazy and sceptical afterthought and where ritual and community are far more important than any theological doctrine, as William James ... argued. The religion of ancient China was like this - that is, with the gods as an afterthought; so too was the religion of Rome. Hinduism, with many hundreds of gods, is for that reason adjacent to Buddhism, with none.'

I have argued that religious propostional belief is over-rated and, at least as far as the doctrine of *karma* is concerned, far from trouble-free. Yet religion may be a source of consolation, a cure for our metaphysical loneliness, a vision of affirmation in a broken world (and sometimes a crippled and corrupted vision, making the world even more broken).

I hope that in writing this book I have been able to shed some light on the way one central doctrine of religion has offered a vision of the world and to offer an alternative way of thinking about life and death.

ABOUT THE AUTHOR

Ian Walker

Ian Walker was born in Sydney, Australia but has spent most of his life in the UK. His doctorate in philosophy at the University of Wales was supervised by Huw Price and DZ Phillips.

He was, for 26 years, Headmaster of one of the world's oldest schools (founded in 604 AD) and has taught in universities in the UK and the USA.

He is married to Kerrie, a mathematician turned lawyer; they have a daughter, Hilary, who lives in Sydney and works in cyber-security.

Ian and Kerrie live in a small, rural village in Oxfordshire and spend much of the year in Australia.

BOOKS BY THIS AUTHOR

Plato's Euthyphro

A commentary on the Greek text of one of Plato's early dialogues

Faith And Belief: A Philosophical Approach

An assessment of the nature of faith in the Christian tradition

The Anatomy Of Belief And Unbelief

Agnosticism and atheism, as most commonly understood, represent a misunderstanding of faith and are grounded on self-defeating assumptions. Apart from its application to religious historical tenets, propositional belief has scant place in religion. Yet trying to recover historical propositions in religion is a fruitless exercise.
In religion, there can never be justification. The unbelief which attacks this misguided notion is chasing a chimera. Faith should be seen as a thoroughly natural phenomenon. Metaphysical atheism is as misconceived as metaphysical theism.

The Number Of The Beast - A William Adams Thriller

Dr William Adams, an Oxford Egyptologist, and Laura Tennett find their lives under threat after the murder of Laura's boyfriend, Jeremy White, a research student whose doctorate Adams is supervising.

While the police seem to be getting nowhere in their investigation, William and Laura escape to a safe house in an attempt to decipher Jeremy's doctoral thesis which may hold a clue to his murder.

They are tracked down by a mysterious organisation operating within the Roman Catholic Church. Their lives are in jeopardy as they discover a secret harboured by the Church for centuries and which threatens to destroy it.

Their travels in England and France lead them to the resting place of one of history's most important caches of religious documents, secured by an ancient sect implacably opposed to the Catholic Church. They discover both the riddle and the solution to Jeremy's death ... and so much more.

The Cylinder Of Babylon - A William Adams Thriller

An ancient clay cylinder, covered in cuneiform writing, is discovered by archaeologists in Babylon, in war-torn Iraq. Prof William Adams is called from Oxford to translate the cylinder and there collaborates with Prof Ellie Green. Further spectacular and widely-publicized finds apparently confirm the history of the Bible.

Terrorist activity forces the dig site to be closed and Adams and Green's lives are threatened.

Adams completes his translation of the cylinder only to find that his discovery could set the combustible world of the Middle East alight. National and international pressure to suppress Adams' findings mount as the cylinder goes missing.

In this dual-voiced narrative, we also learn of the travails of the original seventh-century BC owner of the cylinder and how it comes to be placed in the secret archive rooms under King Nebuchadnezzar's great library.

Loved By The Gods - A William Adams Thriller

A sensational discovery in outback Australia leads English academic William Adams, Visiting Professor of Archaeology at the University of Sydney, and his team to investigate.

A chance meeting draws the team into the ambit of the Mangarai, custodians of the country on which the discovery is made.

Tensions develop as the operations of the archaeological team, the Mangarai, Ernest Souter, 'owner' of the land, and would-be developers of the uranium-enriched site, clash.

Two stories of the tribe and team are interwoven as kundela-initiated murders follow abduction and rape.

Vengeance, it appears, is never satisfied.

The M Galaxies Trilogy

Science Fiction

Three books in one: three planets, three murders, cosmic consequences.

Book 1: Lyra - The M57 Galaxy

Science reaches its natural conclusion: the extension of human life to infinite duration. But is the price too high to pay?

On an outworld mining planet, a mysterious scientific institute experiments on bio-replication with fatal consequences.

Book 2: Hyadea - The M45 Galaxy

In a remote, vulnerable village, happenstance determines that all the children become telepaths who come to unite two continents and to dominate life on the planet.

Book 3: Ilium - The M45 Galaxy

The ancestors of the telepaths are now the greatest power in the Supercluster. They find that their hegemony is threatened by newly discovered, neolithic men.

Printed in Great Britain
by Amazon

33a02288-5239-4605-8a10-4095d7f82839R01